A Persuaded Heart

**Discovery House**

P U B L I S H E R S

BOX 3566 · GRAND RAPIDS. MI 49501

*PUBLISHING BOOKS THAT FEED*
*THE SOUL WITH THE WORD OF GOD.*

# A Persuaded Heart

*Gladys M. Hunt*

*A Persuaded Heart*

First published as *Ms. Means Myself,* copyright © 1972 by Gladys Hunt

Revised edition copyright © 1991 by Gladys Hunt

Discovery House Publishers is affiliated with Radio Bible Class
Grand Rapids, Michigan

Discovery House books are distributed to the trade by
Thomas Nelson Publishers, Nashville, Tennessee 37214

**ISBN: 0-929239-41-5**

Unless indicated otherwise, Scripture is taken from the
HOLY BIBLE, NEW INTERNATIONAL VERSION.
Copyright © 1973, 1978, 1984 International Bible Society.
Used by permission of Zondervan Bible Publishers.

*Printed in the United States of America*

91 92 93 94 95 / CHG / 10 9 8 7 6 5 4 3 2

# Contents

# Preface

A woman's life no longer follows a given pattern. Stereotypes do not fit the woman of this decade. A whole new world of opportunity has opened for her, and many voices compete for her attention.

When walls that have defined a person disappear, life can seem unsafe. It is still an uneasy world out there. Women are doing things they never did before, including going to war and fighting along side of men. Roles offer some protection; when roles no longer seem relevant, choices have to be made that can make or break us.

It may be an uneasy world, but it is also an exciting time to be a woman. Freedom is always exhilirating. Some people are fearful that it is also dangerous, and they are right. The danger lies in the choices that need to be made. Will women use their new freedoms wisely?

The excesses that immediately follow new freedoms have already spent themselves for the most part. Women, so eager to "have it all," have found that some of what they wanted isn't worth the price they are paying for it. They have seen the results of their choices. The liberal faction is still trying out shocking lifestyles and a few keep on shouting slogans, but the women's movement on the whole has lost its steam. It is doubtful that women will retreat to their former role-oriented life, but the venom has been taken out of the rhetoric which at one time was either compelling or upsetting, depending on your life's circumstances.

Some issues still need confronting. For some people old

stereotypes die hard. When men still see women as sex objects, rather than persons, more education needs to take place. However, women have shown an ambivalence about this issue, which also demands some education. Many give themselves away too cheaply, send mixed messages, and are themselves confused on the values of life.

A good marriage has taken on more value than it had for a time. Most college women remain career-minded, and are willing to marry later and put off having children so that they can try their wings in the marketplace. Some carry this too far. One forty-year-old woman having her first baby said to me, "I didn't know if I would like being a mother; now I think it might be the most important thing I have ever done!"

Her reluctant motherhood came from the unhappiness and brokenness of her family background. We can expect to see generations of young people groping in their own marriages and with child-rearing because of the hurts that have come from the excessive divorce rate of the last two decades.

Still women want families, and the size of families is even increasing. A balance is returning to life. But choices still have to be made about quality life, and quality is my concern in writing this book.

Quality life is always the result of making the right choices. Many voices compete for a woman's attention, and life on the fast-track can blur the significance of our choices. Sometimes we don't see the big picture—the immediate pressure focuses our attention on the minutia of life.

This book focuses on your inner life and the choices facing you. It reminds you of what is really important, of what is genuinely valuable. God's point of view, His resources, His promises, His practical help—that's what I have written about. I am convinced that the One who made us is the best qualified to help us through the maze of life.

I am grateful to all the women who have shared their lives with me and trusted me to understand—friendships in the student world, in rural communities, in suburbia, and in a university community. I have seen in their lives the struggle, the beauty, and the challenge of being women in a complex world. Their lives have illumined my own; sharing God's truth with them has made it more true for me.

*Gladys M. Hunt*
*Ann Arbor, Michigan*

# I

# THE GOOD NEWS
# ABOUT YOU

Everybody has to feel good about themselves for some reason. The need is built-in. It's part of being made in the image of God. God meant for Adam and Eve to have a sense of well-being—not pride, but a feeling of worth and ability. He so honored this first man and woman that He allowed them to choose. In the cool of each day He came and talked with them. He gave them responsibility to care for the Garden of Eden. God provided this man and woman with all they needed to "feel good" about life.

Everyone knows only too well that something destructive happened to the man and woman. As Creator, God provided abundantly. As creatures, they were given only one limit. Only one tree in a garden full of trees. They were not to eat of it. When they chose their own way instead of God's, all sense of well-being disappeared. They wanted to hide their bodies; they wanted to hide themselves; they began to blame each other for their dilemma.

The disorder that began in Eden plagues us to this day. Life seems designed to exploit our feelings of well-being. Competition, selfishness, an emphasis on the physical instead of the spiritual—life seems distorted. We either end up feeling unsure of ourselves or we become skilled at proving something to ourselves about ourselves.

Nothing is as great an impediment to getting along with others as being ill at ease with yourself. Self-acceptance is crucial to accepting others, and it is a necessity for living with yourself. It is not humility that makes a person exclaim, "I don't like me!" or "I can't do it." It is rather a destructive root of unbelief about self and personal worth that has its roots in the folly that took place in Eden.

Robert Frost once said, "Nothing scares me so much as someone who is scared." We know what he means because we have experienced that too. It is a negative cycle set in action. Another's fear binds me in some peculiar way and I react instead of acting as a free agent. Suddenly I lack spontaneity. Her self-consciousness makes me self-conscious, and I must struggle to free myself from the web of her restraint.

The person who cannot accept herself sets in motion myriads of negative cycles. When she sends out negative impulses, the reactions she receives confirm her self-view. Because surveys reveal that contemporary women rate low self-esteem and depression as their most serious problems, I think the issue needs to be addressed head-on.

Negative people are hard to live with, no matter who they are. If you have ever met Eeyore, the gray donkey from the Winnie-the-Pooh stories, then you'll know what I mean. Eeyore lives in a gloomy corner among the thistles of the Hundred Acre Woods, a corner that matches his personality. When Pooh says, "Good morning to you, Eeyore," he replies, "Good morning to you, too, Pooh. If it is a good morning. Which I doubt." He is almost totally absorbed with his own moods. He rarely moves out in positive action toward others, and is almost accusative when someone acts positively toward him. He adds hilarity to the stories because of his ridiculous self-consciousness and the ludicrous postures others take to reassure him of his worth. When we read about Eeyore, everyone laughs because we know people like him!

In this way, people with low esteem seem to live against others, rather than for others. When Miss Low Self-Esteem enters a room full of people, she automatically assumes no one will like her. Or perhaps certain kinds of people will not like her. She projects her view of herself onto others. Her self-defense is often to decide that she doesn't like any of them. So there! It's a cover-up for expecting rejection. And it probably means that she has never learned to trust anyone in all her life!

Her chances for natural friendship are gone before she begins. Entering with a negative idea, she proceeds to collect available data to confirm her self-view. Negative feelings take on many hues. "He will not find me interesting." "I am not a good conversationalist." "Everyone is more sharply dressed than I am." The list is as varied as any person's insecurities. No matter how or why she does it, the end result is a terrible kind of slavery to self. People who think lowly of themselves usually think too much about themselves.

Low self-esteem usually has roots in our past: rejection by someone important at a critical stage in life; love given as a reward for performance; a repressive lifestyle during childhood; comparisons within a family; family status in a community—all can produce a pattern of internalizing or living warily in relationship to others. When the antenna is always out to bounce off others, we take our self-view from how others react to the signals sent out. This is a disastrously self-defeating process.

Pressures from the world heighten a sense of worthlessness. Knowledge increases so rapidly; we can never know all there is to know nor keep up with new trends, new ideas, or even a current vocabulary. What's "in" can drive anyone looking for security to utter despair. The consumer rage, "You'll attract him if you use —— product," or "To be successful, try ——" undercut any simple sense of security. A person can begin to feel, "There is no place for me."

Add to this all the trivia published about women today, and you've entered into a cult of feminine uncertainty. To wear ruffles or to strive to be president of the company—or both? On one page of a journal is an article about the kind of women men like; on the next page is a stirring assault on male chauvinism. One psychiatrist writes about bargaining with your children and not repressing their independent spirit. In another magazine of the same month a study commission reports on permissive parenthood and its effect on juvenile delinquency. One article shouts out "Who Needs Men?" And another tells you how to capture one and get him to the altar.

But it's not womanhood that is basically at stake here; it is personhood. The struggle to accept one's self and have some identity is the cornerstone for building a meaningful life. We must come to terms with personal worth. Who can tell us who we are and what we are worth?

God can. He is the major presupposition on which this book is built. In the final analysis, His is the only opinion that counts. He is the Creator and Sustainer of the universe. He is the ground of our being. He is the all-powerful, all-knowing, ever present Love. He is ultimate reality. He is the perfection of fatherhood. And He has told us about our value; His actions have demonstrated our worth; His daily concern verifies our personhood. Who we are is best defined by *whose* we are. Discomfort and unrest fade when we know God as Father.

We have grown used to the phrases people use to define

value. *Her father is worth a million dollars. She has made worthwhile contributions in that field.* The crowd-stoppers, the celebrities, the producers—these are worthwhile. And then some scientific buff tells us that the chemical value of a person is about $3.71. Inflation. It used to be 98 cents.

The fact is that the world's standard of worth has become so much a part of our thinking that we have trouble hearing and understanding what God is saying to us about our value in His sight. God has openly declared our personal worth at Calvary. To question His declaration is unbelief, not humility.

Everyone needs to visit Calvary for two reasons: (1) to see the awfulness of our personal sin that necessitated the death of Christ and (2) to see that God thought we were worth dying for. Both are necessary if we are to understand anything about God's love. Emphasizing either one to the exclusion of the other weakens the value of one. Understanding both is to comprehend the good news of the gospel.

Many people have just enough religion to make them miserable. They believe in a God who takes sin seriously, who has reminded human beings of moral failure, but they stop there. Keenly aware of inadequacy, they live in the slough of despond—worthless, sinful, guilty. They find no comfort in God for their lack of self-acceptance. His verdict only confirms what they already know about themselves. They may say they believe their sins can be forgiven, but God's love is conditional. It is based on an if. *If* love allows people to experience little freedom from their feeling of inadequacy. They are more conscious of themselves than of God.

Ellen had this kind of a problem. She had recounted a troubled childhood to me. Her mother died when she was fourteen, and an overly busy father took over the reins of the household. No one had time to listen to Ellen's needs or to understand her loneliness. So she sought comfort elsewhere—with older boys who claimed to love her but who only used her. Each time she felt the ashes of no love, of exploitation, and declared it would never happen again. But her personal need made her vulnerable in this area.

During her freshman year at a university she met a girl who told her about God's love and forgiveness. It was bigger than anything Ellen could ever imagine and she hungered to know God and be loved by him. She spoke of her faith in Jesus Christ and of God's forgiveness. But in reality it was a long time before she really accepted the forgiveness God offered her. Her sins were always before her. She needed constant reassurance from others as to the value of her person. Fear that she might slip again plagued her. Then she would lose God too.

Often this kind of misery over self is found in homes or churches where strong teaching about sin is regular fare but where the freedom Christ offers is seldom mentioned. The psychological bent of a person may cause her to hear only verses that speak of "denying yourself" or "hating your own life" or "in my flesh dwells no good thing." These phrases feed an already developed low self-esteem and are taken out of context to add to her woe.

Phillips Brooks once said, "The true way to be humble is not to stoop until you are smaller than yourself, but to stand at your real height against some higher nature that will show you what the real smallness of your greatness is." I like that. It is true to the teaching of the Bible. God has declared our value, our personal worth. He created us with our present genes; He can redeem all of the experiences that make our life. So stand up tall; give Him all that you are. We do not need to fuss over ourselves. Boasting is excluded when one is in proper relationship with God.

Others progress a step further. They know God loves

them and has accepted them, but are quite sure that He loves them *because* they have trusted Him and because they do their very best to be as good as possible. *Because* love is risky. Given an imperfect action, the love disappears. But even worse is the high standard of performance for the wrong reason. He loves *because.* People caught in this trap usually come from backgrounds where love is given on the basis of performance, and withheld if there is disapproval.

I am increasingly convinced that a major cause of the despondency, the ineffectual living, the lack of freedom, the feeling of worthlessness so common in today's world is a failure to understand what God has done in redeeming us—and how and why He has done it.

Recently I heard of a postage stamp that was auctioned off for $205,000. It was a small piece of paper scarcely 3/4 of an inch by an inch. I would never have paid such a price for such a thing! But its value did not depend on my feelings. Its value was found in the heart of the man who was willing to pay such an enormous price for it.

Just so our value does not lie in our own feelings. It lies in what One was willing to pay to redeem us. God declared our value at Calvary. Your value. My value. He said openly, "I think you are worth dying for!" God said that. If you doubt your own worth, you are disputing the God who made you.

That's the good news the Christian has to share. You are loved. God loves you. He sent his Son to Calvary to take care of your sin problem—the sins which make God seem so far away from you. God offers to save you from your sin, your self, your inadequacies, your depressions— because He loves you. He offers this redemption as a free gift, but a gift has to be received to be a valid gift. And receiving this gift involves a personal confrontation with the living God. Being a Christian is not merely believing a set of truths or being a moral church-goer. It is establishing a relationship with the God who loves you, who has designed you to live in fellowship and harmony with Himself.

God means for His children to live with an enormous sense of well-being. He made it possible for us to be free from all our old hangups and the opinions that bind us. He constantly assures those who trust Him of His steadfast love. "You shall be mine, says the Lord Almighty, in the day when I make up my treasured possession." He calls us His children, and we enter into the wonder of the Fatherhood of God. He promises His continued presence with us: "I will never leave you nor forsake you." He tells us not to be anxious because He knows all our needs. His resources are available to us as we trust Him. Those who come and eat at His table are satisfied.

The apostle Paul demonstrated this as he wrote from prison, "Rejoice in the Lord always." His letters ring with a sense of well-being. Yes, he is conscious of sin. He described himself as the chief of sinners, but quickly he went on to rejoice in the deliverance of the Lord. Yes, he was pressing on to the prize of the high call of God in Jesus Christ, but not because God's love was dependent on his striving. God's love was his source of joy and freedom even in prison. He declared that we are more than conquerors through Him who loved us.

What we are getting to now is a basic understanding of what justification is all about. *Justification* is one of the most important concepts in the Bible. It is not common to our vocabulary and therefore needs explanation. Translators of modern English editions have struggled to find an adequate synonym and have failed. A word study of *justification* requires paragraphs if we are to comprehend its marvelous truth. Translating the word with the phrase "put right with God" conveys only part of the truth.

Salvation means being justified. Justification is a declaration by God; it is a legal act. We are declared righteous by God. It is not something that results from what we do, but rather something that is done to us. God regards us as righteous the moment we exercise faith. Furthermore, He declares us righteous even though we deserve His wrath. We bring no goodness to Him which makes His declaration necessary. No, He acts on our behalf because of Calvary. The only action we can take is one which makes it personally effective for us—our individual faith.

Often when a question is asked about the meaning of justified, someone will define it *Just-as-if-I'd never sinned.* That's a neat little handle, but like many simplifications it doesn't convey the whole truth. It is as inadequate in defining God's action toward us as the house, swept clean but left empty, mentioned in Jesus' parable. God does not treat us simply as if we had never sinned; more than that, deserving His wrath, He gives us his righteousness. Not a slate wiped clean, but a slate inscribed with the righteousness of Jesus Christ.

Furthermore, justification does not mean that we are made righteous in the sense that we are no longer conscious of sin. Justification makes no actual change in us; it is a declaration by God concerning us. Failure to understand this puts people on a spiritual roller coaster ·and our misunderstanding is the devil's hey-day.

On any given day you may be conscious of failure, of having disappointed yourself and God. You find yourself thinking, *Now I've done it. God has turned His back on me. In fact, I am going to have a hard time restoring His approval of me.* And if you believe that, you turn to wallow in your failures, knowing discouragement and defeat. You are sure you are going to have to do penance or work very hard at the Christian life to be acceptable again. It's the devil's lie.

Your condition does not yet conform to your position. Your position, if you are a Christian, is this: declared righteous by God. The whole process of the Christian life is to grow, to change so that our condition is more and more conformed to our position in Christ. The Bible calls this sanctification.

That is why it is so important to understand justification. Doubts come about ourselves. We must turn from ourselves to see God's verdict. Yes, He has pronounced us guilty. We do not take this lightly. "The wrath of God is being revealed from heaven against all the godlessness and wickedness" (Romans 1:18). But God has done something about our guilt. We see both His justice and His love at Calvary. And we read and believe one of the most important verses in the Bible: "They are justified freely by his grace through the redemption that came by Christ Jesus" (Romans 3:24). Declared righteous by faith.

If God accepts us, are we not insulting Him to fail to accept ourselves? "Since we have been justified through faith we have peace with God," Paul writes in Romans 5:1. Why not peace with ourselves as well?

I am not talking about an egotistic self-love; I am talking about the kind of self-acceptance that affirms our personal worth and frees us from the prison of self-absorption. When we need constant reassurance about our personhood, we have set self at the center. The psalmist reveals the secret to mental, spiritual, and physical health so beautifully: "I have set the Lord [not self] always before me; because he is at my right hand, I shall not be shaken. Therefore my heart is glad and my tongue rejoices; my body also will rest secure" (Psalm

16:8-9). Notice that the heart, the mind, and the body—the whole person—is affected by this perspective.

Our problem with reflecting on self is that our thoughts either lead us to self-praise and self-satisfaction or plunge us into discouragement and despair. Whichever it may be, inevitably any view of God is shut out and we lose the wonder of being justified. When we get hold of what it cost God to justify us, and the love that led Him to do it, our self-view takes on biblical perspective. God has redeemed us; we can lift up our heads and shout praises. God's love is an *in-spite of* kind of love—love that is safe, that lets us dump our load honestly before Him, assured of His constancy.

Why is justification so important to understand? Because it is the only worthy ground of our own self-acceptance. Your family may have given you an adequate self-concept by their support of your personhood, whether they claim to know God or not. But the spring of their ability to do that is the love of God revealed in Christ even though they do not know this. In contrast, you may come from a scarred background. Whether your battle in self-acceptance will ultimately be easier or harder than the person from a secure background depends on your openness to receive and believe. Perhaps you will appreciate the value of justification more fully because you are more desperate to do so. Someone has said that there are no super-Christians, just super-receivers. Regardless of background, God offers us the freedom of knowing our personal worth is bound up in His character. He believed we were worth dying for; He declares those who believe justified! "They are justified freely by His grace through the redemption that came by Christ Jesus" (Romans 3: 24).

This verse is like John 3:16 in conveying the message of our salvation. We have already spoken of the meaning of being justified. Notice other important words in these verses:

grace, gift, redemption. All three words indicate that we have done nothing to deserve being declared righteous or justified. It comes to us freely, as a gift of God, in response to our faith. Not everyone receives the gift, but those who believe are justified.

*Grace* is a wonderful word! Grace is the exercise of the spontaneous love of God. Although we deserve His wrath, He chooses to give us His love. Notice that it is *His* grace. Grace comes only from the heart of God. But it cost God something—the redemption that came by Christ Jesus. Because God is holy and just, something had to happen before our forgiveness could become possible. Our sins were paid for by the death of Christ. He ransomed us. Our redemption came to us through Christ Jesus. Thus, Paul goes on to say, God proves himself to be both just and the justifier of all who believe in Jesus.

Understanding this led Martin Luther to pen:

Lord Jesus, Thou art my righteousness
I am Thy sin;
Thou hast taken upon Thee what was mine
Thou hast set upon me what was Thine;
Thou hast become what Thou wast not
That I might become what I was not.

This is what it means to be made free. "It is for freedom that Christ has set us free," Paul wrote to the Galatian Christians. God wants us to be free to be who we really are. Yet so few have entered into His freedom. Meeting a woman who is genuinely free to be herself, with her hangups dumped at the foot of the cross and acting without self-consciousness, is so rare an experience that it scares some people into a corner. Such a woman is the norm for Christian womanhood.

She may not be average, but she is normal. And God wants to raise our averages.

What is such a woman free to do? She is free to love God. She is free to love others. Appreciating that God took the initiative in our redemption—and keeps on taking the initiative in individual lives—she is free to follow his example. She reaches out to others on the basis of love, not only need. She is free to forgive because she knows herself forgiven. She accepts herself because God has accepted her.

Lacking this freedom, some women are like tightly closed buds, atrophying on the vine. Afraid to open up, they do not dare risk the bloom lest it be less beautiful than someone else's.

Others become harping critics, quick to point out error in someone else and slow to love. Others don't criticize, they just internalize, never letting anyone know who they really are. They don't risk exposure or love or acceptance. Some play games, wearing the mask of a role they have chosen, sometimes a very spiritual role. Those are outwardly pious and inwardly barren, still unknown to anyone else or themselves. Others talk too much, skirting all the issues which might reveal their real person. And still others become authorities on any subject, even Bible-quoters, to hide blatant insecurities.

Increasingly women are trying to prove their personal worth by achieving in the marketplace of the world. Honors, paychecks, positions, beauty—any bid for recognition can soothe the nagging doubt and keep us from facing ourselves. It is at this very point that our concern for rights for women may lead us astray. Issues of fair opportunity, employment, and paychecks are important. The creation mandate to "subdue the earth" was given to both female and male, and vocationally there should be no closed doors for women who have the ability and the calling to pursue a given field of study. But when all the doors are open, we will still have the human problem of personal worth. We are not equally gifted; we do not have equal opportunities even within our own ranks. Each woman is different. The woman who possesses the epitome of what other women long for still faces her lonely, uncertain self.

To define our worth by giving us new things to do, better jobs, or larger paychecks is still to miss the heart of our need. Our worth is not bound up in the position we hold, in what we do, or in what we own. That may only be a new kind of bondage, fraught with competitiveness and comparisons.

We make our own prisons. God's invitation is to come out. Knowing some restless, seeking woman, ill at ease with herself and with her world, I have often thought, *She needs to sit on the Lord's lap and let Him love her and quiet her a bit.* I have sat there often myself and come away refreshed in my own person. It's the Lord's promise, you know. "As a mother comforts her child, so will I comfort you" (Isaiah 66:13).

# 2

# THE SIDE ISSUE

We might say Adam was the first Freudian because he traced his problem to sexuality. He looked at the state he was in and complained to God about the woman God had given him. Men and women have been blaming each other for their troubles ever since. But sexuality is God's idea, and for all the flurry over the male-female controversy, no one can imagine life without it.

Sexuality is not synonymous with sex, as this word is used today. The sexual aspect of life unfortunately is often reduced to the sex act, something almost apart from our persons. Sexuality is far more encompassing, and our failure to understand this impoverishes us. We are sexual beings. The very fact of your human existence means that you are a sexual being. Sexuality is part of the divine creative order; it is personality incarnate as male or female.

That's obvious, you say. But I would go beyond that to say obviously *good*. Not just a fact, but a positive contribution to life. Sexuality is not tacked on to selfhood but belongs to its essence. Sexuality is the way I express who I am to others. In that sense, everything I do is sexual because I am a woman. To be a woman is a total way of existing.

God made the man, placed him in a garden, and invited him to participate creatively with the Godhead. Man was given the privilege of naming all the creatures God had created. It was serious business, for the Bible says that whatever Adam called the animals that was their name. That kind of partnership in creativity never fails to excite me. Imagine the thrill of Adam's task.

But, the Genesis account continues, Adam found no one of his kind in all creation. He was alone. God knows the joy of unity because he experiences this wholeness within the Trinity to an extent that we cannot understand. In fact, oneness is God's idea; it is a God-concept. Knowing the joy of completion, of oneness, of fellowship, God declared that it was not good for man to be alone. So God fashioned someone like the man in kind, yet different in function. A person to complement and complete Adam. He recognized immediately that this was "bone of my bone and flesh of my flesh." He called her woman because she was taken out of man, and he received her joyfully. Then follows a most important and beautiful verse defining marriage, a verse quoted by Jesus and Paul in the New Testament: "For this reason a man will leave his father and mother and be united to his wife, and they will become one flesh" (Genesis 2: 24).

Humanity is both male and female, not one or the other. Genesis 1:27 reads, "So God created man in his own image, in the image of God he created him: male and female he created them." It is important to note that when both male and female are created the text speaks of their being made in the image of God. A unity. Mankind, as opposed to animal-kind. Together male and female represent man made in the image of God. Together they are given dominion over the earth.

The generic term *man* includes woman. The word *Adam* also means mankind, as in Genesis 5:2, "Male and female he created them, and he blessed them and named them Man [or Adam] when they were created." The creation account clearly and profoundly links male and female into a unity. Far more than being a "helper," woman is essential to man's being, and he is incomplete without her. Priority of creation *may* indicate male headship, but there is no evidence of superiority as there is no superiority between the first and second persons of the Trinity. As the Son was to the Father, so woman is to be to man (1 Corinthians 11:3). The two, male and female, are side by side in creation.

We often think in terms of masculine and feminine characteristics. Both are found within the personality of God. God is both male and female in that sense. Male alone was incomplete. A fuller representation of God's image necessitated female. Man and woman together represent the image of God.

Therefore, I believe it is superficial to say that the difference between the male and the female is merely physiological. If that were the only difference, it would still not be so "mere," since a woman's physiology permeates and conditions her daily life more directly than a man's does. In fact, it is one of the burdens many women resent. One thing seems obvious: Woman is not a man with feminine features anymore than a man is a woman with masculine features. A common humanness exists, which includes mental and spiritual equality, but God had more in mind than procreation when He made male and female.

Woman is a separate creative act of God. She is like the man and yet different. She has proven herself to be the equal of man, but that is different than being equal to or the same. We err if we overemphasize sameness, and we fall into a trap of another kind if we specialize only in differences. Suffice it to say here that woman brings different gifts to the world, and this observation placed into experience has been the joy and conflict of many lives.

I labor over this because some of the currents of thought today begrudge the idea that God should be spoken of as a male. Some even object that the term *mankind* is prejudiced against women. God is Spirit. He is represented to us in ways which we can understand, and thus he is spoken of as God, the Father. Personally I find the Fatherhood of God a vastly comforting experience, and it seems to me that all that is implied in his Fatherhood is found at the core of the universe.

If we are personally diminished by the male reference to God, we have not begun in any way to come to terms with our own sexuality. God made me a woman, and although all the world were to be male-dominated and oppressive, I believe He expects me to carry my womanhood with dignity and honor because it is not inferior in His sight.

The divine design is no mistake. The mutual attraction of male and female calls us out of our aloneness, out of our independence to see that we need each other. It is the foundation of human history. We are meant to enhance each other, to affirm the other's personhood, and to discover that in our mutual dependence we solve the mystery of our existence.

Obviously, something has gone awry in the relationship between men and women. The unity, the complementing, the enhancing has become the rare experience rather than the normal. Absorption with sex as a commodity or an experience has dehumanized both men and women so that an act becomes more important than personhood. Sex clouds our appreciation of sexuality. Sexuality belongs to the essence of our person, and if this were properly understood we could be content with an emphasis on accepting ourselves as persons.

Perhaps because I am a woman I believe that women suffered the greatest loss as the result of the fall. I have speculated on Satan's strategy in making his approach through the woman. Was there something inherent in her nature that made her more receptive to his deceit? And was there likewise a receptivity to his wife that influenced Adam's behavior? Whatever the answer, a disaster took place. Both the man and woman hid themselves from the presence of God. This simple sentence—both tragic and profound—is the key to understanding subsequent history.

Everything changed for both the man and the woman. Henceforth the man would toil to obtain his food all the days of his life, the very ground of the earth working against him. Thorns, thistles, the sweat of his face. Sin's disorder more directly affected the woman's person. Childbirth would be painful; her own body would work against her. Her desire would be for her husband and her husband would rule over her. Sin was let loose in the world. Selfishness. One-up-manship. Exploitation. Domination. Fatigue. Unrest. Abuse. Deceit. The misery of meeting self's needs. The loss of identity.

Conceit and moral perversion led men away from God's ideal in the mutual creation of mankind. Men began to see women as inferior and for their own use. The farther men went from the divine revelation, the darker the picture for women. Her loss of prestige and her rightful place beside man degenerated steadily, and history indicates that the darkest years came after 1000 BC. One of the first indications of this decline in the Bible is found when Lamech took two wives. Polygamy was never sanctioned by God and directly opposes the principle found in Genesis 2:2. God receives considerable blame from contemporary feminists for the subjection of women. Blaming God for mankind's troubles is consistent with our perverse nature; the subjection of women was born out of sinfulness, out of the fall.

A study of history reveals that the ancient Hebrews, in contrast to the pagan nations around them, never completely lost the ideal God had given them at creation. In the Law, for instance, children were instructed to honor both father and mother. Women of excellent spirit rose to prominence and national leadership in Israel. A woman was a judge, some were poets, and others were leaders. One thinks of Esther, Miriam, Deborah, Huldah, and others. Even the power of a wicked Jezebel shows the extent of women's influence in Israel. History records that Queen Alexandra during the inter-testamental period initiated compulsory education for both boys and girls, a revolutionary concept at that time, thus banishing illiteracy in Palestine. Yet the Old Testament also records discrimination against women, the adoption of pagan practices, and the prophets' outcry against the desecration of marriage (Malachi 2). The Bible is very honest in recording wickedness.

The desire to dominate, to subjugate another, to be superior comes out of the heart of mankind set in opposition to God. We have only to think of galley slaves in Mediterranean ships to realize that women have not been the only ones to suffer. In fact, wherever women have been able to maneuver the situation, they have dominated men with a variety of weapons, leaving their own mark on history. But when a Jew prayed, "I thank thee that I am not a woman," he was not reflecting the viewpoint of God anymore than the contemporary church does when it expresses prejudice. It seems natural for mankind to try to find someone to look down upon. And others take pride in "looking down on those who look down on people."

Even at the height of their culture, a low view of women existed in the Greek and Roman worlds. Noble women are mentioned, as well as businesswomen like Lydia, but only in Greek art and poetry are women heroines. Aristotle is said to have taught that women were inferior in every way, only a rank above slaves. Xenophon, the historian, recorded these prejudices and wrote that women are best kept confined to an "inside world." Plato advocated community wives. Goddesses, fertility rites, and prostitution in pagan temples scarred the lives of both the men and women to whom Paul preached in Gentile cities. In the city of Corinth, for instance, a thousand prostitutes were kept in the temple as part of pagan worship. Without question, the life of the early church was complicated by the experience of the people in it, and this is the context of Paul's teaching about women and the problems of marriage. First Corinthians 7 must be read in light of the entangled relationships which existed in a new church born out of such a culture.

But light comes to the darkness. God becomes incarnate in Jesus Christ to restore mankind to Himself. The Son of God confines Himself to a woman's womb and is dependent on her care and nurture. In that one event alone God signaled women's status. Mary's song is a song of enablement by God. As Jesus becomes a grown man He moves about in the company of women with a freedom unknown to the teachers of His day. Even His disciples marveled that He, a teacher, should hold a conversation with a woman in public. And to that very woman (see John 4) He gave the first revelation that He was the Messiah. He was direct and natural in His manner with women, never stooping to a patronizing or domineering role.

Jesus regularly taught women the Scriptures, a practice not normally allowed in Judaism. He commended Mary for taking the "male role" in sitting at His feet and listening to His teaching. He refused to force her into a typical stereotype when He told Martha that Mary had chosen that better part. In fact, He treated both of them as persons who could exercise their own priorities.

In Jewish tradition a woman was not permitted to bear witness. Jesus deliberately broke that tradition and commissioned women to be the first witnesses of the resurrection. He said, "Go, tell the disciples . . ." He also broke the taboo about the ritual uncleanness of a menstrous woman by curing the woman who had an issue of blood for twelve years. He did not simply cure her quietly, but called public attention to the fact that she had touched Him, and He did not shrink from her touch.

When a woman called out, "Blessed is the womb that bore you and the breasts that you sucked!" Jesus rejected that limited view of women and affirmed a greater view of personhood by replying, "Blessed rather are those who hear the word of God and keep it!"

A careful reading of the gospels reveals that Jesus sought to give equal dignity to women in many ways. When He wanted to illustrate how much God loves lost people, He told three parables. In the first, the shepherd, who leaves ninety-nine sheep to seek the lost one, represents God. In the second parable, a woman seeking a lost coin represents God. In the third, a father longs for his son, and the father is God.

Unquestionably Jesus made a sharp break with contemporary culture by giving women full dignity and freedom as persons. Women were not only the first to believe, but were honored with some of the most significant revelations about Jesus. He is Christ, the Liberator, restoring us to God and offering to redeem our prejudices, our failures, and our position in life.

Because of him Paul could write, "There is neither Jew nor Greek, there is neither slave nor free, there is neither male nor female; for you are all one in Christ Jesus" (Galatians 3:28).

Years have passed since His coming. The patterns of sin are deeply ingrained in our society. The abuses of the past have left many women with a loss of personhood, of self-value. Bible verses quoted out of context to prove that woman's existence is for man continue to excuse man's selfish use of and domination of women in some circles. It is appalling to think that as late as the early 1900s women were treated as second-class citizens, without the right to vote, to hold property, or to go to court. If a girl did not marry, few careers were open to her. Time has erased many of the prohibitions of the past, and yet women still must crusade for equal pay for equal jobs. The opportunity to enter almost any profession, including serving in the armed forces, now belongs to women. Yet in many places women still feel discriminated against, and the church is often one of those places.

The church reads the magnificent tribute of a king to his mother in Proverbs 31 on Mother's Day, and then the rest of the year overapplies the transcultural significance of Paul's instructions for women to keep silent. They forget about Philip's four daughters who prophesied and about Priscilla, a co-worker with Paul, who taught Apollos and whose name is often mentioned before that of her husband in the work of the church.

That's the background of the world in which we live. Meanwhile, women have not always been examples of godliness in the face of this stress. Their strengths and their gifts have been twisted out of shape. The instructions of the New Testament that irritate women today were necessitated by real-life situations, interestingly as real today as the day they were written. "And not only do they become idlers, but also gossips and busybodies, saying things they ought not to" (1 Timothy 5:13). ". . . give the enemy no opportunity for slander" (v.14). Paul was helping churches in a pagan world to see that those who believed in Jesus were to have conduct worthy of the gospel. And one of the things that most impressed the first-century world was the honor and chastity shown within the Christian home and the integrity of interpersonal relationships. The pagan Libanius is said to have exclaimed, "What women these Christians are!" That same witness is needed today.

Suffering from exploitation, women have found ways to exploit others: manipulation, playing the distorted female image for all it is worth. Accepting your sexuality precludes this kind of behavior. Men alone have not made women sex-objects; women have let them do it. While seeming to resist, they respond to all the clamor of sexual come-on by the products they buy and the way they act. I've watched women with good minds and high ambitions stoop to the silliest of maneuvers, turning their backs on their best friends, to gain what they thought was that experience of supreme value—the attention of a male.

At the other end of the spectrum are the scared ones who can endure no healthy, wholesome friendships with men. They cut themselves off into exclusive friendships with their own sex, and repudiating the natural attraction between men and women, they grow prudish and become a type of atrophied humanity.

Neither of these have accepted their sexuality and found fulfillment in their personhood. A healthy freedom shines out from the one who can celebrate the joy of being a woman. Shout it out. This chaotic, tension-filled, sex-oriented world has plenty of room for a free and joyous acceptance of womanhood. Redeemed womanhood has a kind of clear, wholesome atmosphere about it that has an uplifting effect on everyone.

A person's attitude toward her sexuality manifests itself in all of her behavior: the way she finds fulfillment, her acceptance of responsibility, her self-discipline, her ability to give herself in relationships, her attitude toward men, and her treatment of other women. The woman struggling with self-acceptance rarely likes other women. She may use them for her purposes, but her loyalty is thin even toward those who seem closest to her. She may avoid women completely and opt to radiate in the presence of men, and thus fulfill a need for approval and identity, but she is wary of relationships which demand anything of her.

Learning integrity in one's emotional life is never easy, especially in the face of the pressures of our present culture, so plastic and pervaded with dishonesty. Yet I feel it must be learned if a woman is to experience the fulfillment and commitment of meaningful relationships.

What do I mean by this? Simply wholeness. Putting it together so that your personhood and your sexuality are in harmony. You've accepted yourself. You have stopped grabbing at life to fill your own needs. You face reality honestly. You can relax and be wholesomely you—not celebrating your hangups, but celebrating the joyful acceptance of being a woman and the freedom to give yourself in your relationships.

The potential for this kind of wholeness is made possible by the redemption found in Jesus Christ. The answer to accepting your sexuality is the same as the answer to accepting yourself. Jesus Christ has redeemed us; He will redeem our personalities, our relationships, our expression of self in the world. He tells us who we are and what we can do. He puts our priorities straight; He fills our empty spots so that we are kept from seeking fulfillment in the wrong places. He understands women. He understands you.

Then why does the Christian church sometimes treat women as inferior, as if they aren't qualified for spiritual leadership? What about those sticky Bible passages about women being silent?

The passages in question come from two main sources: the letter to the Corinthians and Paul's letter to Timothy at Ephesus. Both letters were written in the context of the Greco-Roman culture where women were given an inferior status and temple prostitution was part of life. In interpreting these letters, we need to remember the difficulty this would pose when women were converted and joined the first-century church.

Elsewhere the Scriptures tell of Phillip's four daughters who prophesied, of Priscilla who participated with her husband in teaching Apollos, and of the large number of women mentioned by Paul in Romans 16 who were active in spreading the Christian message. For example, Paul mentions two women (Philippians 4:3) who contended at his side in the cause of the gospel. Paul's accounts of the role of women in the early church are astounding in light of the place women had in the culture in which he lived. We can hardly conceive that the early church fathers would have written as they did on this subject if they had understood the significance and magnificence of Paul's instruction that a man love his wife as Christ loved the church!

But Scripture has been read with cultural prejudice over

the centuries. The early church fathers were more strongly influenced by Artistotle and Xenophon, the major voices of the Green culture, than they were by Jesus' attitude toward women or Paul's writing about marriage. Tertullian spoke of women as "the mother of all ills." Chrysostom wrote of women as "a natural temptation and desirable calamity, a deadly fascination," almost as if woman were designed by Satan instead of created in the image of God. Thomas Aquinas betrayed his prejudice by agreeing with Aristotle that "woman is a misbegotten male," a statement that hardly honors God as the creator of both male and female in His image. St. Augustine agreed with the Greco-Roman tradition that a woman's sole function was procreation. In fact, I find the writings of the early church fathers on this subject appalling. We are still saddled with remnants of this biased interpretation of theology.

The cultural attitude to slavery was similar. Paul told Onesimus, a newly converted runaway slave, to return to his owner, but by doing this he did not condone slavery. It has taken many years for society, with a growing Christian influence, to break the chains of slavery. And still there is prejudice. Paul wrote so clearly that Christ had come to break down all barriers: Jew—Gentile, Slave—Free, Rich—Poor, Male—Female. He told Ephesian Christians that God is without partiality.

Prejudice is passed on from generation to generation. The interpretation of difficult passages of Scripture is also passed down to us, sometimes without fresh investigation of the text. We need to continue to search for truth and to ask hard questions, with humility and careful scholarship. We need the grace to admit that we might be wrong in our opinions. What is spiritual leadership, and what is repressive, egotistical domination? Is spiritual leadership only serving as an elder in the church, or as a pastor? Can a woman be a pastor? Were women pastors of churches in Paul's time? What kind of leadership represents Christ's care for the church? Why did God give women exceptional gifts of teaching and administration, as well as high intelligence, if they cannot be used in the church?

Have we taken *relational* words like *submission* and *head* and made roles out of them? Do we stereotype people in ways that Jesus did not? Are we afraid to trust the Holy Spirit in each other? Do we have two levels of spirituality—one for men and one for women?

The weight of biblical emphasis gives godly women more freedom than most have yet realized. The problem is godliness and the godly exercise of gifts by both men and women. Women are not captive to ancient culture; they are captive to God and His working in them.

A person can be many things at once. To say that one thing is true about any person is not to say that some other trait is not sometimes also present. A given trait does not make one inferior or superior. The Hebrew word for man, *ish,* means strong. The word for woman, *ishshah,* means soft and delicate. On the one hand, that is a matter-of-fact observation. On the other hand, we can make from this such rigid stereotypes that a woman can never be an initiator, a man is never tender, and both come out with a cookie-cutter regularity that defies reality. It is hard to believe this is what a creative God planned for us.

Differences exist between men and women. Both can be cooks, tailors, teachers, lawyers, doctors, or business people. Both sexes are capable of performing a variety of kinds of work and doing so with equal intelligence. However, that is not to say that both will react the same way in the same situations. If one person arrives at an answer intuitively and another rationally, that is no comment on which way of reaching a conclusion is best.

At the risk of being misunderstood, I do believe a different pulse beats in the veins of a woman. Emotionally they look at the world differently. Women have been gifted by God with special sensitivities and gifts—and responsibilities—in the emotional realm which enhance human relationships. Her attention to detail introduces color, harmony, joy, lightheartedness into human life. Berdysen remarks that woman is the doorway to community, that she has a civilizing effect on the world.

Ah, you say, I know men who are sensitive to others too. So do I. And I know women who are not. That does not invalidate the generality. Nor do I think of these as rigid categories that confine women. I believe they enhance her self-appreciation. They need to be emphasized because we are losing what the world needs in our strain to be equal. Equality is not what women need, but the right to develop to our fullest potential to be what God wants us to be. And the last phrase of that sentence is important. The job we do may be relatively unimportant; what we are is critical.

Commenting on the difference in the sexes says nothing about intelligence or ability to think—or inherent value in spiritual terms. I am not complimented when I am told that I think like a man or drive like a man. For me a man is not the standard. I am a woman. The best of femaleness is the standard.

But we strain too much on this point. Once we've accepted femininity we can get on with being a person— a feminine person. Feminine defined is simply that pertaining to being a woman. It's not the ruffles we wear, it's the person God made us. And expressions of femininity will vary with our genes and ambitions, but they will be feminine because that is what we are. Feminine can mean continuing to grow, tapping the potential of our minds and hearts as well as our wombs. It can mean rejoicing in the force of life within us and being present in every moment in all that we do.

Do not let others poison your joy in being created female. The possibilities inherent in being made woman are as creative as the God who made us. And there is great dignity in His design.

# 3

# ONE STEP FROM EDEN

Doing your own thing is "where it's at" these days. It is especially "in" for women, who recently have been revealed to be the largest oppressed group in the world. Everyone needs to express themselves, to have a little elbow room to discover new dimensions of their personalities. Affluence allows it. The climate of permissiveness encourages it. A contagious fever rages. The voice of selfishness is heard in our land.

No, I can't really take a church school class. You see I've got a season-pass at Summit Ski Lodge, and I go there every weekend I can . . . Well, skiing really does do more for me than teaching wiggling sixth-graders on Sunday morning, don't you think? I find it more fulfilling.

Could my son be in your Cub Scout den? . . . No, I can't help. You see, I work . . . Yes, I wanted to use my training instead of letting it go to waste. And I just love it. The only problem is that it takes me away some evenings . . . No she's only two, but I drop her off at a babysitter . . . Why yes. Would store-bought cookies be all right?

The Retirement Home? Well, I'm no good with old

people at all. I'm afraid I just couldn't. Besides I'm spending all my free time making a new wardrobe for my trip to Greece this summer . . . Yeah, Marge and I are going. It's our third summer abroad . . . Well, I really am sorry I don't have time to help.

I just couldn't take it any longer. After all, being confined with two pre-schoolers gets pretty dreary. You get so you just long for adult company . . . Well, Tom helps me with the housework in the evenings, and it really works out quite well . . . Sounds interesting, but I don't have time to read. I hardly ever find time even to read to the kids.

Well, the weeks go by fast. On Monday nights I wash my clothes, on Tuesdays I wash my hair. Wednesdays I usually go home and have dinner with my parents so I don't have to cook a big meal. Thursdays I clean the apartment and on Fridays I go home again. I usually sleep in on Saturdays and then go shopping for clothes with my mother or my aunt.

No thanks. We just enjoy being by ourselves. We don't like the inconvenience of having to entertain others back. We usually spend the early evenings watching television, then have a glass of milk and go to bed. It's peaceful and quiet with just us two.

I watch our kids being neglected, and I can't do anything about it. I want to finish my degree and she's determined to finish hers. She asks what right I have to do it if she can't. Actually, we're very competitive. She won't give in and let me be first, and I won't give in and let her be first.

It's kind of a stalemate in leadership, and our children suffer for it.

Conversations like these are as varied as the people speaking. And none of them are really wrong, morally I mean. Couldn't good motivation prompt their point of view, factors we don't know about? I mean, after all, it's their decision.

But we are also "deciders," and we need to ask ourselves if there is something eccentric in today's freedom to do your own thing.

Responsibility has become almost a dirty word. A bit Puritan and repressive. Freedom and responsibility seem to oppose each other. Hardly anyone asks, Am I free enough to be responsible?

Significantly the Bible says little about rights, but much about responsibility. Freedom is a dominant theme, but it is the freedom offered by Jesus Christ—freedom from sin, from self, and from unworthy choices. In fact, a potent warning says, "You were called to be free. But do not use your freedom to indulge your sinful nature; rather, serve one another in love" (Galatians 5:13). That's biblical freedom—freedom to love and serve someone else.

Freedom is a staggering concept—easier to talk about than to experience. Its counterfeits are many. How many enticements to freedom have led people into a grim kind of slavery rather than into the adventure they sought! Genuine freedom is the great adventure, because it links us up with God who is prime Innovator and Creator. It is quite different from doing "your own thing."

Personal freedom demands that we choose the quality of our adventure. In fact, we must decide what our adventure will be. We cannot give ourselves to two adventures at the same time. We must decide what is worthwhile. Too many people live with divided hearts and their lives are fragmented with a little bit of this and a little bit of that. None of it fits into a meaningful pattern, and the person, having made no decision and no commitment to what is worthwhile, wastes years—or a lifetime. An ironic tragedy is to aim at nothing and hit it. Or perhaps worse still, to aim at the wrong thing and hit it.

I have sometimes thought that I'd like to be a dozen different people. One of me could be an interior decorator and I could spend someone else's money as an exciting outlet for some flambouyant ideas I'd like to try out. I'd like to be a professor. I'd like to be a foreign correspondent or teach overseas. Whenever I go into a restaurant that has an extra touch of charm, I think it would be fun to run a cozy place that is not run-of-the-mill.

I'd like to be a partner in a business with my husband because I think he is clever and it would be fun to dream and plan together. I'd like to write a column for a newspaper. I'd like to sail around the world in our own sailboat. You name it—I'd probably think it would be fun to try. But alas, I am only one person. And with my one life I must determine the most valuable way to spend it in the will of God.

Deciding on what is worthwhile demands having a standard, a measure outside ourselves. On what basis will you judge what is worthwhile? The principle of pleasure has proved an unreliable guide. "But I enjoy doing this" hardly passes as a statement of value. The principle of success has seen more than its share of catastrophes. Paul Tournier says, "Every one of us feels that there is a hierarchy of choices, that a person can succeed in many things without believing his life worthwhile."

What is worthwhile must have meaning in an

ultimate sense, in God's sight, so that all the small pieces of each day, though they be trivial, will fit in with that meaning. Existence is not absurd, as Camus would have us believe. It forms part of a coherent plan laid down by the Creator. Our personal choices or adventures are only significant as they are in harmony with the adventure or plan of God.

Furthermore, every choice of what is worthwhile necessitates that we reject some other good possibilities. Robert Frost reminds us of that.

> Two roads diverged in a yellow wood,
> And sorry I could not travel both
> And be one traveler, long I stood
> And looked down one as far as I could
> To where it bent in the undergrowth . . . .
>
> I shall be telling this with a sigh
> Somewhere ages and ages hence:
> Two roads diverged in a wood, and I—
> I took the one less traveled by,
> And that has made all the difference.[1]

What is good is not necessarily worthwhile for me. Good can crowd out best. A profession, a mate, a course of study seem to be critical roads to us. But the same principle applies to the small choices in life. They must fit into a larger picture.

Skiing is a good thing. But going every weekend may not be worthwhile. Intellectual interests outside the home are commendable, but if they cause neglect of the people I love most, they are not worthwhile. With mobility and affluence, some people live at such a fast and hectic pace that they have never discovered life's other possibilities. Possibilities like peace and quiet for meditation, family sharing, and listening to God. The question is one of long-range goals that fit into the will of God, of thinking beyond our present experience so that life is not haphazard, but meaningful.

Women have never had so many choices, but that has not assured that their lives will be more worthwhile than when they were imprisoned to home and hearth. We may just be rushing to get the front seat on the bus without knowing where it is going. The outcome can resemble a woman let loose for the first time in a fashionable store; a bit of this and a little of that, but none of it fits together to make an outfit. An orange floppy hat with pajamas! Like a small girl trying on her mother's clothes; it's only funny when you are little. Because when you grow up and make irresponsible choices it hurts others besides yourself.

Furthermore, we tend to ask such small questions about our role in life. For instance, students ask me, "Do you like housework?" I suppose they ask that because it represents the epitome of slavery to them, and because they seem unaware that any commitment has its less exciting moments. I never ask myself that question. It is irrelevant. It is akin to asking a student if she likes to study, or a man if he likes to drive to work. Housework is only a small part of a larger picture I am painting with my life. Does an artist like cleaning her brushes? I don't discuss the pleasure of housework—I do it. And yet questions like these often mark the small talk of women. Are we that confused?

Do I like housework? And who will be influenced by my life? These are two different kinds of questions. If I answer the latter, I may more gladly accept the former. Our problem is that we often do not even know when questions are not of the same value. Hence, we have difficulty fitting short range goals into long-range satisfactions.

Discovering what is worthwhile changes our orientation to life. We can feel called or appointed to a role in life, instead of chafing at the bit or feeling used. Less consumed with being fulfilled, we are free to fulfill our calling. But this necessitates the kind of acceptance of personhood that we have been discussing. It requires real freedom.

The confusion and tragedy of the Women's Movement may be that women are being led to think that children or the confines of marriage are the cause of their personal frustration when the root cause lies deeply within their own personhood. The diagnosis is wrong and the result is wasteful and destructive.

"The victim of this confidence game believes with all her heart that her only satisfactions are going to be those earned by leading an independent life, remaining loyal to abstractions, and doing her own thing. She cannot allow herself to believe that these misty ideals may actually be substitutes for the give-and-take of intensely personal relationships and extended personal commitments—where love is not something you go around talking about but something you do."[2]

On the other side of the fence stands the single woman who believes all her problems would be solved if she had the love of a good man, children, and a home in which to express her creative talents. She may be unaware that she longs for this man and these children, not to share with them the richness and satisfactions of her own life, but to make up for all that is empty inside her. She, as well, may reveal an incapacity to give of herself in interpersonal relationship.

Many of the illnesses people suffer express this kind of dissatisfaction with life. It is a cover-up for lack of commitment and the freedom to see beyond immediacy. No decision about what is valuable, what is meaningful, no commitment to God or to others is paralyzing.

Fulfillment is not so much trying something new as it is coming to terms with your present situation. God, who is creative, may add a splash of color here and a new experience there, but it will always line up with your responsibility to fulfill the commitment made.

A little boy once said to the housemother of his boarding school, "You are kind, but you do not love us." Not only little boys are perceptive about the loving ones. When someone is living for self, disinterested, limping along without commitment, she announces it to the whole world by her priorities and behavior. The common expression "Her heart is not in it" comes to mind. When a person commits herself to what is really worthwhile, she becomes part of the flow of the love of God. And her heart is in it.

How do we get our hearts into it? We begin by going to God.

". . . Faith, far from turning us away from the world brings us back to it. That is why it awakens in us a new interest in the world, in the concrete reality of every day, hard, laborious, difficult, often painful as it is, but wonderful nevertheless. The joy of living, of making an effort, of having a worthwhile goal to aim at; the joy of moving a finger—of looking at something, of hearing a voice, of learning something and loving someone."[3]

Loving others puts our hearts back into the stream of life.

It is worthwhile and valuable. It is full of fresh surprises and new discoveries. Loving is our responsibility. We have the example of God who commits Himself, who is not passive in His responsibility but charges Himself with our personal care. This kind of godliness on our part marks our fulfillment. It gives us enthusiasm (the feeling of God inside us) for living. It changes the mundane, the trivial, so that in all circumstances of life goodness reaches out to others.

If this is your thing, do it with all your might.

# 4

## Shaping Up

Crying is all right in its way while it lasts. But you have to stop sooner or later and then you still have to decide what to do. When Jill stopped, she found she was dreadfully thirsty. She had been lying face downward, and now she sat up . . . she listened carefully and felt almost sure what she heard was the sound of running water.

The woods was so still that it was not difficult to decide where the sound was coming from . . . Sooner than she expected she came to an open glade and saw the stream, bright as glass, running across the turf a stone's throw away from her. But although the sight of the water made her feel ten times thirstier than before, she didn't rush forward and drink. She stood as still as if she had been turned into stone, with her mouth open. And she had a very good reason: just on this side of the stream lay the lion . . .

"If you're thirsty, you may drink . . ."

For a second she stared here and there, wondering who had spoken. Then the voice said again, "If you are thirsty, come and drink . . ." It was the lion speaking. The voice was not like a man's. It was deeper, wilder and stronger; a sort of heavy, golden voice. It did not make her any less frightened than she had been before, but it made her frightened in rather a different way.

"Are you not thirsty?" said the Lion.

"I'm dying of thirst," said Jill.

"Then drink," said the Lion.

"May I—could I—would you mind going away while I do?" said Jill.

The Lion answered this only by a look and a very low growl . . .

The delicious rippling noise of the stream was driving her nearly frantic.

"Will you promise not to—do anything to me, if I do come?" said Jill.

"I make no promise," said the Lion.

Jill was so thirsty now that, without noticing it, she had come a step nearer.

"Do you eat girls?" she said.

"I have swallowed up girls and boys, women and men, kings and emperors, cities and realms," said the Lion. It didn't say this as if it were boasting, nor as if it were sorry, nor as if it were angry. It just said it.

"I daren't come and drink," said Jill.

"Then you will die of thirst," said the Lion.

"Oh dear!" said Jill, coming another step nearer. "I suppose I must go and look for another stream then."

"There is no other stream," said the Lion . . .

It was the worst thing she had ever had to do, but she went forward to the stream, knelt down, and began scooping up water in her hand. It was the coldest, most refreshing water she had ever tasted. You didn't need to drink much of it, for it quenched your thirst at once . . .

"Come here," said the Lion. And she had to.

Thus C. S. Lewis tells his allegory of the "shaping up" of

Jill in his book *The Silver Chair.*[1] Jill had been a nasty, competitive pain-in-the-neck before she met Aslan. That encounter made all the difference in her life.

That's the first step in "shaping up" for any woman—meeting the Lion, quenching your thirst and feeling suddenly safe. You may try other streams, but there are none. And you drink at his invitation. Jesus' invitation is, "If any one is thirsty, let him come to me and drink. Whoever believes in me . . . streams of living water will flow from within him."

An encounter with God and entering into a personal relationship is not the same as being religious. Passionately religious women may still not know God. Emotionally they experience lofty thoughts that make them feel good; ideas about God stimulate them and they affirm their belief in Him. Something is missing. It is the encounter—the personal relationship—that makes the difference. God wants to free us so that we can get on with life.

Some women have managed to shape up and ship out into the mainstream of life, handling the currents and the rapids and the quiet pools with a gracious, confident ease. Others are trapped in one eddy after another, going nowhere at all, hung up in swirling pockets of confusion. Everyone gets sidetracked once in a while, and requires a rescue operation. That's the way life is. But some have been caught in an eddy or on a piece of dead wood for so long that they have forgotten that life was meant to be lived in the mainstream.

Too many people are weighted down with appendages and loads they were never meant to carry. We are our own worst enemies. We harbor the ugly and neglect the good. Too early we lie down under the burden and say, "That's just the way I am." *I am so foolish. I am good-for-nothing. I am full of fears. I am so bad-tempered. I am weak in this area. I am jealous.* Our lives are full of wretched I ams that spell failure. The *I AM* that can rescue us is the *I AM* of God. He says, I am the all-sufficient One. Remember when the people of Israel, in bondage to Egypt, asked Moses the name of the one who would deliver them. God said, "Tell them I AM has sent you." God's name is *I AM* and behind that *I AM* are all the resources we need. He says, "I am your peace. I am your strength. I am your deliverance." His *I AM* cancels out our failures.

Below is a list of words that describe different kinds of women. Look it over carefully. Check off the combinations that describe you.

Scared and frigid
Nervous and demanding
Warm and loving
Callous and thoughtless
Boisterous and nervy
Pessimistic and small-minded
Gabby and short-tempered
Sensitive and self-conscious
Always right and misunderstood
Perfectionist and rigid
Wise and understanding
Sensual and undisciplined
Complaining and unthankful
Jealous and possessive
Thoughtful and appreciative
Fearful and uncertain

Which of these burdensome realities would you like to unload?

You can be different. That is one of the joys of knowing God. We are not stuck with what we are. Many of us are like the woman who was walking to the market in town carrying a heavy load on her back. A friend came past in a wagon and offered her a ride. The woman thankfully climbed aboard, but still sat there bowed under the weight of the burden. Finally her friend said, "Why don't you put your load down on the floor of the wagon?"

The woman replied, "It's very good of you to take me to town. I couldn't ask you to carry my burden too." We need God for disasters, for the final moment of death, but isn't it asking a lot of Him to help us get rid of our measly, uncomfortable burdens?

I am reminded of a story that Corrie Ten Boom told of a journey she took into Amsterdam with her father as a young girl. Her father had purchased a suitcase full of parts for his watchmaking business and when the train was nearing their home station, he asked Corrie if she would like to carry the suitcase off the train. She was eager to try, but could move it scarcely an inch. Then her father wisely said, "Remember, Corrie, there are some things too heavy for you to carry. You must give them to your heavenly Father, just as you must let me carry this case off the train." In the years that followed when Corrie was interned by the Germans in a concentration camp during World War II those words came back to her often, and she would pray, "Father, this is too heavy for me to carry. I will give it to You."

The starting point is admitting to the symptoms that make our lives diseased. Dis-eased, that is. Some may be overly sensitive and wondered if they didn't have all the negative traits on the list. Others read it over and checked off only the positives or else skipped over it completely. Why the difference? The first case could be a low self-concept or an overly eager attempt to be honest. The second could be self-protection or an inability even to evaluate one's own person.

This is why it is so important to have daily fellowship with God where your spirit is tuned in to listen as you read the Bible and pray. God is a good teacher. He points out one thing at a time for us to work on. When we feel like a confused failure who needs to be changed all at once, the source of our feelings is not God, but our enemy. God will help us deal with one item at a time. He puts a gentle finger on first one thing and then another and suddenly we have insights into ourselves that we never had before. The person who never has a new insight either has no hangups—or she isn't listening!

Look back over the descriptive list of personality types. How many of these could be taken care of if you simply believed God loved you? Believing this would give you a different self-concept and potentially free you from many habits. But it isn't a push-button cure. You believe and then you must take a stand repeatedly on what you believe. Thoughts come to you, and you resist them and say, "I will not feel that way because I know . . ."

A second question. Looking back over the list, how many of these *might* be eliminated if your physical condition were different? Maybe your thyroid is out of whack. Or you are suffering from anemia or some other malfunction. I learned long ago to inquire into people's physical health when dealing with spiritual problems. One affects the other, and it works both ways. Fearfulness, uncertainty, sensitivity, nervousness can cause physical problems. In that event, the solution is a spiritual one. On the other hand, a rundown physical condition can cause spiritual problems. Some people need to see a medical doctor and take some hormones or an iron pill. Others need the discipline of more sleep and a slower pace.

A third question: How many of these traits stem from just plain old-fashioned sinfulness? Self-centeredness is the cause of at least half of these traits. It's the opposite of being filled with the love of God. Any time we are more conscious of ourselves than we are of others or of God, we are in a trap, an eddy that keeps us out of the mainstream of life as it ought to be lived.

What's the solution? It is found in the Beatitudes. We begin by recognizing spiritual poverty. *Blessed are the poor in spirit.* We mourn because we are so poor in spirit. *Blessed are they that mourn for they shall be comforted.* We realize that in ourselves we cannot become what we need to be; we need God's love to fill us. *Blessed are the meek.* We hunger and thirst for God Himself. *Blessed are those who hunger and thirst for righteousness for they shall be satisfied.* Hungering and thirsting for God changes our whole set of priorities, our viewpoint, our lifestyle. God fills our hearts with His love when we are hungry to know Him. We are changed by a spiritual exercise born out of intense desire to be rid of a most disfiguring burden—self-centeredness.

It hurts to face your sins. Admitting that you lose your temper or get angry is hard on the ego. If you mean business about cleaning up your life, you'll have to learn how to ask for forgiveness and say, "I'm sorry" to others—your husband, your children, your mother-in-law, your friends. If you are really sorry for your lack of control, you'll stop rationalizing about what caused it and how you couldn't help yourself and earnestly ask God to quiet your insides and work out patience in your daily experience. And you'll learn that at the moment when the flare-up is being ignited you can turn instantly to God for strength and control. "Oh, Lord, calm me down. Give me Your perspective. Fill me with Your love." And He will.

We can't forget the woman who gets a great psychological boost from telling someone off, and then recounting her cleverness in lengthy descriptions to others. "I really told her," she says. It may be a business deal, a child's teacher, a fellow employee, but whoever or whatever, the abrasiveness of the situation makes the rest of the world cringe. Some people collect resentments and outrages. I think of the Lord Jesus who was right and righteous, and how people marveled at the gracious words He spoke. When the boisterous, the aggressively nervy, the always-right, the bellicose come into His presence they must hang their heads. God wants to provide amply for inner needs that cause us to act in these ways. He wants to take care of our need to feel superior by making us like Jesus Christ.

Some people are angry at God. Perfectionists often are, even though they won't admit it. Life hasn't been neat and tidy and the way they planned! Anger at God is a symptom. The basic problem is unbelief. God isn't in charge, or if He is, He blew it. Which says not so much about God as about them. Perfectionists want to be God's chief counselors because they don't believe He can do it without them.

Unbelief is the most disastrous of all our attitudes. It keeps us from coming to God for the resources we need. We don't believe He can produce the goods! We are not sure He is completely trustworthy and so we try to limp along pretending a faith we haven't realized. Unbelief makes people sick mentally, physically, and emotionally. A painful lot of the mental and emotional uncertainties experienced by many could be solved best by learning how to believe and how to cast one's self on the goodness of God.

The biggest burden carried around is the load of guilt. It drags us down with a steady pull. For how many people does a simple theft return again and again to haunt and destroy inner peace! I recently heard someone tell how she had knowingly accepted two one dollar bills stuck together when she had only been entitled to the payment of one. For twenty years she had felt unclean over that incident. Whenever she came close to God, this miserable memory made a barrier. Finally with the encouragement of God through reading the Bible she decided to be done with it once for all. She first confessed the sin to God and asked forgiveness, and then she wrote a letter, returning the dollar bill with an explanation. It was only a dollar bill, you say. No, it was a theft, and what a costly load it made. Twenty years of guilt that was unnecessary.

Restitution cannot always be made for mistakes we make, but where it is sensible it should be done, simply because it is right. And it is a therapeutic purging. However, if our attempt to make restitution causes more hurt than help, it can be the selfish therapy of unbelief that makes our actions more important than God's. When God has forgiven us, then what is crucial has been done. This is especially true in the area of sexual sins where some women feel constrained to confess all when the end result is only further hurt, not healing. God's forgiveness is enough in instances like these. And if no one else is involved in our wrongdoing, then the one to tell is God, not the whole world.

Do you know the quality of God's forgiveness? The Bible says, "As far as the east is from the west, so far has He removed our transgressions from us" (Psalm 103:12). "I, even I, am he who blots out your transgressions for my own sake, and remembers your sins no more" (Isaiah 43:25). "I have swept away your offenses like a cloud, your sins like the morning mist. Return to me, for I have redeemed you" (Isaiah 44:22). "If we confess our sins, he is faithful and just, and will forgive us our sins and purify us from all unrighteousness" (1 John 1:9). He removes our sins; He blots them out; He will not remember them; He sweeps them away; He cleanses us from all unrighteousness. Why would anyone hang on to sins when such provision is made for their disposal?

People cripple themselves with both the memory of the wrong deeds they've done and the deeds done against them. God offers to dispose of all our guilt and wipe clean our memories. He offers forgiveness. When we accept it, we are suddenly more free than we have ever been to forgive someone else.

Is there any kind of sin He will not forgive? None, except the ultimate refusal to come to Him, which denies the Holy Spirit's ministry to us. People worry about the unpardonable sin instead of coming to Him to be pardoned. Some would make sex sins the next thing to be unpardonable, but God lists them along with gossiping and coveting. The Bible says that sex sins have serious consequences because they are sins against our own bodies and affect another's body as well. But no one needs to wear a scarlet letter A and be so presumptuous as to think they can make atonement for their own sins. Christ died for our sins. He invites us to confess our sins and be forgiven. Healthy people are forgiven people and forgiving people.

I emphasize this because many people enjoy wallowing in the past, reviewing their sins and almost revelling in the sorrow of their guilt. Others forget everything else except the sins of others. Spiritual health is forgetting what is behind and pressing on to the mark of the high call of God in Jesus Christ.

Some sins become habits, like lying. Isaiah the prophet wrote about this long ago. He said, "We have made a lie our refuge, and falsehood our hiding place" (Isaiah 28:15b). The liar has a quarrel with life; it isn't good enough as it is. Lying thus reflects on the character of God. People lie because of low self-esteem, to get attention, to take advantage of someone else, to destroy them, and for a variety of other unfortunate reasons. Lying makes no sense because it usually hurts the liar most. But that is characteristic of sin. Lying means you have to keep your lies straight, which seems a terrible trouble unless you live in an unreal world. Jesus called the devil the father of lies.

The best way to beat the lying habit is to confess your lies to the people to whom you have lied and ask their forgiveness. Nothing is harder on pride, but if you mean business with God He will help you break out of this trap by facing the consequences of lying. Then if you ask Him, He will be your constant, present help to keep you from repeating the habit.

Confession to others helps break any habit, because it asks for human support in your weakness. If the habit is a private one, the encouragement of one loyal friend who has the integrity to help you may be a tremendous boon. For example, confessing our fears to a friend gets them out in the open where they can be looked at honestly. Most of us think no one else ever feels as we do, and we are surprised to discover that others really understand. And sometimes when things are out in the open they seem less serious than we thought in private. Another person can hold us to our intentions and help us break habits as well.

Jealousy is one fear that prompts a lot of foolish behavior. Some jealousy is petty and stupid; *she spoke to her first, not to me* or *their son was chosen last time.* Or the second wife who is jealous of a father's love for his children and does all she can to drive them apart, thus managing to make a loveless home. Some mothers can't let their children belong to anyone else at marriage, and some children can't let their parents remarry. The Bible calls jealousy covetousness, which is the same as idolatry. It's a matter of worshiping at the wrong shrine again.

Other jealousy comes from deeper hurts: a husband who flirts or whose business is suspiciously monkey business. God knows how unfaithfulness hurts, so go to Him and get your strength and comfort there. Ask Him how to handle the situation—whether to confront or keep your hurt a private affair. It may be good also to take an inventory to see whether anything in your life has made it easier for your husband even to think unfaithful thoughts. Obviously no one is perfect, but we can be too busy, too tired to love, too unconcerned with his world, too careless in our appearance—and make the temptation of someone who isn't too tired or too busy more appealing.

Here is where your prayer life will prove the power of God. In fact, if your life together is lived in the Lord's presence with integrity, and if you are praying honestly together with each other, unfaithfulness is an unlikely event. And especially if your husband does not share your personal faith in God, your prayers for him may keep him and bless him in ways he will never understand. But a careful life must back up your prayers.

No matter how we rationalize in the end, sinful jealousy turns out to be a manifestation of unbelief. It is the opposite of a faith point of view. It must go to the rubbish heap with the rest of the trappings we collect that keep us from really living life.

Feeling neglected you may have some temptations yourself. It's a free-swinging world that says only happiness counts, that if something makes you happy then it is good. Nonsense. Our lives must reflect the character of God if they are to know anything about the real stuff of happiness. *Happy are those who hunger and thirst after righteousness, for they are satisfied.* And it is of inestimable worth to grow old liking yourself and having no regrets.

A word about temptation, any temptation—the temptation to swear, drink, be angry, sleep too much, be unfaithful, lie or shout at your children. God has made provision for every kind of temptation. "And God is faithful; he will not let you be tempted beyond what you can bear. But when you are tempted, he will also provide a way out so that you can stand up under it" (1 Corinthians 10:13). Others before you have been tempted as you are. No one needs to be swept away as a helpless victim. Claim this promise and memorize it. But you will have to do more than memorize a promise; you will have to utilize the way of escape he offers. That means calling what is wrong exactly what it is: sin. We must not justify our wrong behavior.

We've scarcely scratched the surface of all our hangups and touchy places that need to be discarded and cleaned up if we are to live as we were meant to live. Paul wrote a good word to the Ephesians when he said, "Live life, then, with a due sense of responsibility, not as those who do not know the meaning and purpose of life, but as those who do. Make the best use of your time, despite all the difficulties of these days. Don't be vague, but firmly grasp what you know to be the will of God" (Ephesians 5 :15 JBP).

# 5

## LIVING CREATIVELY

Two little brothers shared the same room, and every night the smallest one fell out of bed, arousing the whole household in his trauma. It happened so often that the events became common breakfast-time conversation. After listening quietly for some time, the older boy finally offered his opinion, "Want to know why Timmy falls out of his bed every night? He goes to sleep too close to where he gets in."

Many people have Timmy's problem. They go to sleep too close to where they got in. Dull of spirit, they feel uninteresting, and act that way too, because they went to sleep where they were, and life has grown smaller and smaller.

If I were to ask you how much wealth you had gained in the last five years, what would you say? Inner wealth, I mean. The furnishings inside that are beautiful, interesting, and enriching to others. Some people are like the two men I saw in a cartoon: one said to the other, "By the time I was smart enough to know where I was going I wasn't going any place."

Of all people in the world, the people who claim to know God ought to be the most creative simply because they are related to the Creator. He is the innovator, the creator, the artist. Imagination finds its source in Him.

Imagine being there when "the morning stars sang

together" as the world was created by the word of His power. He shaped birds with their various plumage; He designed the hippopotamus and the giraffe. Light, dark, sun, moon, water, sky, clouds, earth, trees—the rose. And man in His own image.

He let Adam be a word partner with Him by naming the animals. He designed the high priest's robe and the mercy seat, and equipped the artisans with His Holy Spirit. He told Solomon how to carve out the lilies at the top of the columns in the temple. This is our God.

God, the creative Redeemer—who invades our planet to deliver us from our sins and the fear of death—comes not with trumpets and royal fanfare, but as a baby. God, the adventurer.

Did you know that twenty-five percent of the Bible is poetry? In the last part of Job, when God speaks He gives thirty-four verses about the crocodile and ten verses to the glory of the hippo. No wonder G. K. Chesterton wrote "God may be younger than we are!"[1]

He has never grown tired of His world. The elements are created in such a way that each sunset is an original and each snowflake is different. Every baby born is a unique person. God is forever creating and enjoying His creation. The worst thing in the world, says Clyde Kilby commenting on the creative process, is to believe that today is like yesterday.

God notices; He is observant. The Bible says He knows when a sparrow falls. Are you not of more value than they? He keeps on creating in our personal lives too. He takes all the mistakes, all the broken places and weaves the threads of our lives into something meaningful, as we trust Him.

True creativity is always linked with God. It is part of the adventure to which God calls us. Just living in fellowship with this kind of God is the greatest of creative adventures.

As we listen and obey, the Holy Spirit infuses into us a likeness to Jesus Christ.

Paul Tournier says, "He calls us to an adventure of faith, difficult and exacting, but full of poetry, of new discoveries, of fresh turns and sudden surprises."

Then why are some of us so small? you ask. Our smallness comes from the desire to "play it safe." Never take any risks. Never make a new decision or trust God in a fresh commitment. We look at our own resources and say, I could never do that. Our scared littleness keeps us in a box.

Adventure or creativity—whichever word you like best—always involves risks. It involves a decision; it is purposeful; it is an expression of yourself. Usually it involves others. It stretches you, so that you end up being more than you ever thought you could be. It adds the special flavor to life that makes you feel that you have a secret with God.

At this point you may be thinking of the composition of an exciting piece of music, or a new harmonic arrangement, or a painting, or a poem. And you've already said, "I can't do that." Then don't do that. Find something your own size. It may be learning how to knit; it may be flying a kite on a hillside with your son and getting the tail just the right length so that it will soar out of sight in the blue, blue of the spring sky.

Creativity is taking the stuff of life that exists and shaping it. It is to be for the moment a spark of communication between God and man, reflecting some small piece of His creative nature.

Some of my adventures do not even remotely resemble painting a picture, but they have been big experiences that demanded creativity and resources I didn't know I had. The first wilderness canoe trip into Canada was one of these. My husband and I in one canoe; our son, Mark, and Bill, one of "our boys," in another. An untried river; the equipment and the right amount of food; the skills necessary for survival. When we came to our first cataract (which looked like a giant waterfall to me), I wanted to turn around and go back. Three men let me know firmly that you don't go back on trips like this; we were committed to the river. Often when there seemed no route suitable for portage, I heard my husband say, "Pick up the end of the canoe and follow me."

The black flies ate my husband until he looked measly; the mosquitoes nourished themselves on Bill until he swelled out of shape. It rained; we fought our way through log jams, paddled for hours through marsh lowlands. But there were other days. The sun shone, and a whole beautiful world was reflected in the river. No sound, except for the song of the wind in the top of the pines, eighty to a hundred feet tall, and the dip of paddles in the stream. Birds—cedar waxwings, Canada jays, yellow warblers, redstarts. The otter, the moose, the sunset over the lake, the loon's call, the softness of decaying forest underfoot, the splendor of undisturbed wilderness. *Lord*, I thought, *You made all of this and it was here praising You long before we discovered it. Thank You for sharing it with us.*

That's one kind of adventure. I wouldn't have missed it! But I would never have gone if I hadn't taken the risk, and I might never have gone if I had known the cost in sheer endurance and misery. Think of what I might have missed!

Some people don't have children because they are too busy counting costs, evaluating the risks, and weighing the odds of failure. They will never know what they missed! No one marveling at a child conceived in love, nurtured in the mother, bearing the likeness of both parents can doubt the worth of that kind of creativity.

Excuse me for placing canoe trips and having children in

the same category, but I meant to observe that some people are scared of anything that doesn't have a certain end and doesn't have all the risk removed. No one can really live like that. Life itself is a risk. Yet I am surprised at the number of people who never try anything new. A new recipe. (It may not be good!) A new hairstyle. (I may not like it!) A new game. (I don't know how to play.) A new place. (I've never been there before.)

> Come weal or come woe
> My status is quo.

We seek a smooth path, without any brambles or stones in the way, a straight way without too much incline that leads us to heaven quite safely. On the other hand, God, the great Adventurer, leads us over high peaks, across rocky crags, up steep ravines, across rivers we thought we couldn't cross, and gets us to heaven all breathless, bearing the fruit of our effort and the likeness of His Son— and fit for royal fellowship.

Eric Berne, author of *Games People Play,* says, "Losers spend their lives thinking about what they're going to do. Winners, on the other hand, are not afraid to savor the present, to unpack their books, and to listen to the birds sing. Losers say *but* and *if only.* Winners are enlightened people who grow rich, healthy, strong, wise, and brave using just three words in life: Yes, No, and Wow."

We need positive attitudes to live creatively. We cannot be encumbered by past failures. The Scripture reaffirms this by urging us to "put off" and "press on." Our sensitive egos may still smart from a risk we took that left us bruised. Bruisings of this kind come most often when the adventures have been our own selfish plans rather than true acts of creativity. But remember God is still the author of new beginnings.

I do not speak lightly of taking risks. For some people, telephoning someone else is a great adventure and risk. Introducing someone can be exceedingly painful for others. These are extremes of the spectrum, but they exist. And for such the status is not so much "quo" as human safety. But we are not left to that. An infinitely creative God wants to take us out of our smallness into an adventure suitable for us. We need a positive attitude to begin. We can do it, by His grace.

I'm thinking of such an adventure in my own life. God had brought a woman into my life who was an incipient alcoholic. When life's dreariness or her personal disappointment became too much, she took to the bottle and was out of sight for days. She became a Christian and her life changed radically, and the community of those who loved her had almost forgotten, if they had even known, about her problem. Then one day a neighbor innocently said something that hit a vulnerable spot in my friend; she was angry and hurt and went home.

The neighbor tried to call, other friends tried to contact her. No answer. Her car sat in the drive, but no one could reach her. On the second day the fear grew that she may have returned to the bottle. It was decided that I was to go to her home. My assignment was a rescue adventure with God, but I was a Jonah at heart. She lived in the country and had two enormous police dogs that usually met the car. I never left my car until she called them off. Would she be there to call them off? I didn't want to go; I was scared; I didn't know what to do once I got there. My husband prayed with me and shoved me out of the house. When I arrived the dogs miraculously weren't outside; I knocked on the door; she answered and fell weeping into my arms, asking, "How do you know if God forgives you?" I was so glad I went!

I did not have a positive attitude toward any detail of the

adventure, but I did have a positive attitude toward God, and that is a good place to begin. And I think the illustration points out one other helpful detail: namely, the role of encouraging friends. We can encourage others to take the risk of living creatively.

A positive attitude is inspired by a spirit of thankfulness. One of the most creative exercises a woman can do is to write a weekly theme entitled, "Why I am thankful." Thankfulness changes our negatives to positives, and transforms our liabilities to abilities. A student once wrote a thankful essay for my friend Betty Carlson. It read, "I am thankful for my glasses. It keeps the boys from fighting me and the girls from kissing me."

We need a positive attitude and a spirit of thankfulness, but we also need to uncomplicate our lives. We build stress into our own lives. I'm not suggesting that we leave the sink full of dirty dishes while we enroll in an art class, but we do need to take a careful look at our lives. The details will be different for everyone, but for most it will mean planning ahead to make our lives more orderly and disciplined. There are only twenty-four hours in any one day; make them as meaningful as possible. We waste useful energy with self-absorption which would be better spent on being creative.

Except for a few who are able to shut themselves off from the world, our creativity must be flexible, not selfish, and subject to interruption. Particularly is this true of women who have children at home. And if you are truly creative, you will consider even the interruptions creative.

Sometimes our creativity passes through times of darkness when some of our dross is being burned off. You may be in one of those times now as you read this. Nothing has sparkled for you for quite a while. Again, return to faith in a God who sponsors personal adventure and He will help you begin.

What might some of these adventures be? It could be as simple and big an adventure as honesty with a friend. No more role playing, but the risk, the commitment to be who you really are. Real honesty requires integrity. There is a fake kind of honesty popular today that lets people think they have the right to tell a person (with a bit of disguised anger) all the things about that individual offensive to them. It's a way of saying, "I don't like lots of things about you, so why don't you do something about it." And it's a neat cop-out for learning to love. Real honesty might well work on an offensive habit with another person out of love, but it won't make another person unduly responsible for personal hangups.

For instance, Sally goes to Anne and says, "I have something against you. I'm jealous of you." What does Anne do? Can she negate everything in herself that makes for the jealousy? No, but Anne can take Sally's false attempt at honesty and make it creative by helping her to bear her own burden before God. That's at least a creative response.

The creative risk of adventure in honesty that I first suggested is that of simply letting yourself be known in ways that are free and constructive for you and everyone else. It will undoubtedly include the interchange of letting others help bail you out of your hurts and doing the same for them. A large part of living creatively is reaching outside of yourself to help someone else.

Learning to listen helps creative living. Listening may well be second only to loving as a creative act. Listening says so much to the other person about her value. (That's why listening to small children is so important.) But listening lets you hear and know the other person, and you may be surprised at the totally new ideas you encounter.

I read recently of a man who said he had never been

bored with anyone. When he began to feel tired of a person, he began to ask, "What is there about the life of this person that makes him so boring?" And by the time he had finished asking questions and listening to them explain themselves he was no longer bored.

The combination of honesty and listening could be a whole new adventure in quality married life for some people. Maybe your husband has never learned how to express himself or share, and you live a lonely existence. If you claim the help of a creative God who designed people with the ability to communicate, and creatively heighten your own sensitivity to your husband, you may be in for one of the biggest adventures of your life. Certainly your prayer life will develop; you'll feel the Holy Spirit controlling your responses; and you will be surprised by more than one miracle.

Never give in to a low quality of life within the home when God, the Redeemer, offers His help. One young wife telephoned to say, "Something has been happening to me. It is as if God told me that if I want things to change I am going to have to keep my mouth shut. So I've been trying, and do you know what I've discovered? When you know God you don't always have to be right!"

Another woman has grown beautiful praying for her family and creating an environment that works with her prayers. She prays, "Lord, help my husband not to be so short with Jimmy. He's so sensitive and he never gets a chance to finish what he wants to say. Help John to be more aware of this." And God does.

Making something new and creative out of family life can be a married woman's great adventure. It can also be the adventure of the single person, because the close interpersonal relationships within any living situation demand His help.

One of my great adventures as a writer has come from the families who share with me how *Honey for a Child's Heart*[2] has launched them into new adventures as families through sharing of books. Writing a book is an adventure of the riskiest sort. But after the pain and loneliness of the actual production, what joy and reward to see others learn to live creatively because I took the risk of adventure.

Setting up a reading program seems so simple an idea that one hardly thinks of it as creative. And yet books can take us on the finest kind of adventure without ever leaving the house. A good adventure takes discipline, and a well-ordered life is necessary for a reading program. Think of the potential for expanded horizons, for creative thinking, for learning something new!

I was talking about good reading to a group of mission candidates recently and one winsome young man told me later in conversation that he was a poor reader and hardly ever read a book. His story revealed unfortunate situations in first and second grade and a move to a new location in third grade where other students teased him about his inability to read. He developed a barrier against reading. He was bright and his mind retained what he heard, but he didn't like to read. It threatened his view of himself. I asked, "Have you ever asked God to help you overcome this handicap and work on it with divine help?" He thought about it for a minute, and then said, "That would be a choice kind of adventure, wouldn't it?"

Both reading and learning to read fit the category of creative living. My friend may never be a speed reader, and what he sets out to do is easier said than done. But so is painting a picture or playing a musical instrument. It will take courage and sweat and perseverance.

One of my friends declares that learning to change the

way you look is a phase of creative living. She says, "God gave you your face; He didn't give you your expression. Why not make it more pleasant?" For others it will be discipline of more sleep, better and less food, or a decision to stop chewing the fingernails.

Every meaningful adventure I have had has involved doing something I believed to be the will of God. I have been pushed out over my head in experiences so many times that I've found myself swimming strokes I didn't know I knew! Everything from a radio talk show to taking a chair-lift to the top of a mountain with the intent of skiing down! I was no pro in either event, but I did have some exciting surprises.

I've used the word *swimming* metaphorically, but it reminds me of a literal swim I once took. Gerry had just come to trust Christ. We were taking an exercise and swim class together at the Y. Following our first day of exercises, we jumped into the pool. She stood there for a minute and said, "I'm scared to death to put my face in the water, but now that I know God, I'll just say a little prayer and float across the pool on my face." She proceeded to do just that! Leaving me, who had known God for some time and who always swam with my head well above the water, standing agape. So I said a little prayer and similarly did a prone float across the pool!

The creativity of doing what you believe to be the will of God will more often have significant spiritual dimensions. It may be taking more time with your children, developing a new friendship, helping someone who is needy, or sharing your faith.

Taking seriously the fact that you have been entrusted with the gospel will bring you your most awesome adventures. Creatively sharing the Good News is a most expanding experience. Each person is unique: each hurts in a different place; the capacity for intake of truth varies. To take the great truths of God's redemption and communicate these skillfully takes creativity. We don't dump a load of truth; we interact. We need the right words, the illustrations that apply, the ability to listen—and God's help. No one can ever grow dull or small or uninteresting who grabs hold of this adventure. We have been entrusted with the truth about God!

Living creatively is as big as creation. Don't be among those who think that all birds are sparrows and that there are two kinds of trees: one with leaves and one with needles. Living creatively means noticing, being aware and alive to the world. It involves an appreciation and drive toward excellence. It involves things, people, ideas. God is noticing all the time. Shouldn't we be just a little more awake?

# 6

# Maturing: Growing Beautiful

Some people have trouble letting the Lord shepherd them. Being wayward and headstrong by nature, we are not always sure we need help. We have our own ideas of what looks like good pasture. And so we wander here and there.

In his *Psalm of Wandering*, Joseph Bayly captures the adventures of proud, small humanness:

"Lord you know
I'm such a stupid sheep.
I worry
about all sorts of things
whether I'll find grazing land
still cool water
a fold at night
in which I can feel safe.
I don't.
I only find troubles
want
loss.
I turn aside from You
to plan my rebel way.

I go astray.
I follow other shepherds
even other stupid sheep.
Then when I end up
on some dark mountain
cliffs before
wild animals behind
I start to bleat
Shepherd, Shepherd
find me save me
or I die.
And You do."[1]

Mercifully the Lord does intervene in our lives when we call to Him and, tasting His goodness, it is surprising that we would ever stray again. Happy are those who keep their hearts fixed on the Shepherd; this is what it means to mature spiritually. The most defeating trait in our lives is our tendency to double-mindedness. We say we believe one thing, but we act on a different principle.

There can be no spiritual maturing apart from eating the food He provides for us. The Bible says that "His [God's] divine power has given us everything we need for life and godliness through our knowledge of him who called us by his own glory and goodness" (2 Peter 1:3). God wants us to know who He is, to understand the dimensions of the salvation provided in Jesus Christ, and to be comforted by the Holy Spirit's presence in our lives. Knowing implies information, experience, and fellowship. God has revealed Himself in the written Word, the Scriptures, and in the living Word, Jesus Christ. We are called to His glory and goodness. It is imperative that we *know* God.

No amount of religious exercise will substitute for

spending daily time studying the Bible, and then talking with God about what we have learned. One of my friends was tucking her small son into bed one night. They had just finished praying together, and he said with sudden insight, "I get it, Mom. God talks to us through the Bible, and we talk to Him when we pray. Right?" Right. Profoundly right. Imagine God's love in revealing Himself, His character, and His works to us in the Scriptures only to find that our wayward hearts are careless in exercise of the privilege of communicating with the eternal God.

An African boy, reading the Scriptures for the first time in his own language, said, "This book makes holes in my heart." God means to change the way we think and the way we act as we respond to what we read. And this reading is no perfunctory ritual; it is interacting with God and it makes "holes in our hearts."

A friend and I had been discussing an issue concerning personal faith, and I read a passage from the Bible aloud to her. She had only recently become a Christian and she interrupted me to ask, "Does it say anywhere in the Bible that after you have committed your life to Christ you can understand the Bible better? Because I am comprehending what you are reading, and I have never understood the Bible before!" She was experiencing the Holy Spirit's ministry in her life. Jesus has promised that the Holy Spirit would take the truths of God and make them real to her (John 16:13-15).

God gives us His Spirit when we trust Christ, and the Spirit's ministry in us is to reveal truth and to enlighten our understanding. It is characteristic of new believers to experience the thrill of this, but it is meant to be the continuing experience of all believers. God doesn't dump character into our hearts; He wants to make our own muscles strong by inviting us to go on in our experience of the knowledge of Him. And He gives the Holy Spirit to us to help us grow in ways that change our lives. Holiness is not sentiment; it is the character of Jesus Christ worked into ours. It is always the result of making the right choices.

Those who take their refreshment daily from the Word of God evidence this in their lives. We don't have to announce to others whether we have spent meaningful time with God; it is reflected in the way we think. When some Christian pours out her heart to me and what I hear is out of tune with the grace of God, mixed-up thinking with bitter or anxious overtones, then I know that the solution to her unrest will be found in an exhortation to believe in God and return to feeding on His Word. This remedy has proved amply true in my own experience with God. If I don't have the right diet, my spiritual life goes askew. My point of view turns away from God to look at situations. Ungodly thinking is simply that—thinking without God.

God spoke through the prophet Jeremiah to warn the people of Israel about their neglect of Him. His words have contemporary impact in defining our failure:

> *My people have committed two evils: they have forsaken me, the fountain of living waters, and hewed out cisterns for themselves, broken cisterns that can hold no water.*
> (Jeremiah 2:13)

Oh, the irony of forsaking the fountain of living water to dig a cistern of our own, only to find out it doesn't hold water! What a colossal waste of divine provision and human potential. And some people hold an empty cup to their lips all their lives.

In Psalm 81:16 God says, "You will be fed with the finest

wheat, and with honey from the Rock I will satisfy you." This is God's provision for us in his person, which is revealed in His Word. He satisfies the needs of our inner being; He guides our lives in paths of truth. He has communicated to us. The Bible is a roadmap to the King, someone once said, designed to get us to the palace instead of the garbage dump.

I cannot emphasize enough the importance of a daily time with God in the Scriptures and in prayer. The way for communication is open, a fact made possible by the death of Jesus Christ. That symbolic tearing apart of the curtain to the Holy of Holies in the temple at the time of Christ's death has given us the privilege of approaching God in Christ's name. We become like those with whom we spend time; we begin to think their thoughts after them. If you want to mature and grow beautiful on the inside, listening to God must be a daily habit.

But listening must be the "hearing of faith" that helps us put truth to work in our lives. It is not an intellectual exercise we are after, but the response that involves the whole person—the will, as well as the intellect and the emotion. We are curious beings. Some people say, "If only I could feel," and in a variety of ways they let their feelings buffet them about. The biblical pattern is always to believe—act—know—feel. In other words, we act on our belief which proves itself in our experience and our feelings line up. For instance, "I don't feel I can love her but I believe I should" includes the element of feeling, of belief, of action. When these are put in the right order the statement becomes, "I believe I can love her (because belief puts the resources of God at our disposal); I will act lovingly toward her; my feelings are changed as I obey God." Belief, action, feeling.

Biblical belief is not simply giving assent to a truth. The Bible says devils believe this way. Biblical belief means committing your whole weight to the truth. It means walking out on a plank, expecting it to hold—and suddenly finding it is not a plank, but the very rock on which existence rests. Commitment to truth is the essential element in belief. If I were to go to a bank and present a thousand dollar bill before the teller, I might say, "I'd like to place this in the safe-keeping of this bank." But if I were to hold on to the end of the bill, she would say in return, "I will be glad to deposit it, but you must let go of the bill." It is not committed until you let go and trust the safe-keeping to the bank.

Paul wrote to Timothy with the assurance that came out of commitment:

> *I am not ashamed because I know whom I have believed and am convinced that he is able to guard what I have entrusted to him for that day.* (2 Timothy 1:12)

I am not ashamed; I have believed; I am convinced. This is the secret to the authenticity and dynamic of Paul's life.

The Christian life involves claiming what God has already given us in Christ. Mv grandmother used to speak of this as "claiming the promises," and that is exactly what it is. Peter wrote:

> *He has given us his very great and precious promises, so that through them you may participate in the divine nature and escape the corruption in the world caused by evil desires.*
> (2 Peter 1:4)

That verse is a promise in itself. It says that we can escape the worldliness which infects us and become more like Christ by claiming the promises of God. And the Bible is alive with promises.

Corrie Ten Boom used to speak of this as "writing a check on the heavenly bank." The resources we need are there for us; we need to cash in on them. She learned the validity of these resources in a Nazi concentration camp and says, "It would not be in the Bible if it were not true." Taking generously from God's provision made Corrie Ten Boom beautiful. When you are over eighty and are truly beautiful, it is not cosmetics that makes it so, but a likeness to Jesus Christ.

*Maturing* defined means coming to full development; maturing in experience means facing reality and learning how to handle what we see.

Life is not as perfect as we would like it; our own actions have added to its imperfections. We had a plan in mind and events didn't go that way. We have two choices: to rebel against the way life is or to draw on heavenly resources, to claim some of the promises that will keep us from the "corruption of passion."

The rebels hit out against life, maneuvering on their own resources, and make their own decisions and improvements to correct the faults they find in life. Sometimes it takes on the guise of great sacrifice: the enduring, martyred woman who has given all for her family and finds not-so-subtle ways to remind them. Other times lip service is given to God, but there is little question as to who is running the show. Rebels feel trapped, make decisions based on self's needs, and get themselves into trouble.

A friend was recounting her own rebellion to me. She had been chafing badly at an assignment God had given her. She knew it was His will for her, but the circumstances did not suit her. She was complaining about this in a conversation with an older friend, hoping for some sympathy. Instead, after listening to the whole tale, the friend said, "Did you know that your rebellion is like the sin of witchcraft in God's sight, and that your arrogance is like the evil of idolatry?" (1 Samuel 15:23). That was hardly the sympathy my friend was expecting, but it was the rebuke she needed. "Suddenly," she said, "I saw God's point of view about my rebellious heart. I had been toying with rebellion, almost delighting in it. Rebellion needs to be seen for what it is!"

On the other hand, we may not want to rebel against reality, but we aren't sure exactly what promises to claim. Or we feebly claim them and make such statements as I have made, "We'll just have to trust the Lord." To which my husband remarks, "Has it come to that?" We end where we should begin!

God has already provided the resources we need; His provisions far exceed our needs. The delight of being daily in the Scriptures is that He guides us to the answers we need; He shows us the principles by which to live; He gives us the promise of His personal care.

I will forever be deeply influenced by something my brother shared with me at the time of my father's death. We were concerned for our mother, and he said, "You know, I was so agitated on the inside and then God showed me something. I was reading in 1 Peter, *Cast all your anxiety on him because he cares for you.* I noticed," he continued, "that in that second phrase cares is in the present tense. I don't have to go looking for God to tell him my troubles, He already knows. And He cares." I thought of the phrase from Romans 15:4, "so that through endurance and the encouragement of the Scriptures we might have hope."

The miracle of claiming the promises of God is that they change us as well as change our circumstances. We learn how to solve tension as the Holy Spirit works out self-control within us. Blessed are those who find out they don't always have to be right. And how pitiful are those who have no self-control, who let their emotional passions, their likes and dislikes rule their lives. They are quick to act and speak, but slow to believe that the Holy Spirit will help them in their weakness and that He prays for them according to the will of God (Romans 8:26).

We find ourselves learning to love others we don't think we could love by simply believing and claiming that "God has poured out his love into our hearts by the Holy Spirit he has given to us" (Romans 5:5). We aren't shut up to personal ability; His resources rescue us. If we act as we should, the feeling will follow. God's great plan is to redeem us by loving us. As His love passes through us to others the miracle of redemption happens all over again. I have known the most loveless, tense situations changed by one person who decided to love with God's kind of love.

Recently I talked with a young wife who resented her husband's involvement in his work and his often thoughtless behavior to his family. As the conversation continued it was plain to see that she shut herself away from him as punishment for his neglect. She became critical, complaining of his time away, of her children, of her home, of everything.

Because her husband was of a carefree, happy nature, this was subconsciously unpleasant to him. He did not know how to grapple directly with the tension he felt, so he avoided it. He stayed away as much as he could let his work justify. The children were trapped; they reacted by being as naughty as they could.

I made only one suggestion: that she begin scattering seeds of praise around in the lives of those she loved. I think every woman ought to keep her pockets full of praise and be eager to cast the seed abroad into fertile ground. I don't mean false flattery, but the kind of thankfulness and appreciation of another's personhood that makes others better people. It's another way to let the love of God be shed abroad in our hearts.

God always encourages us; He never discourages us. Discouragement is catching, like a dreadful plague. When the twelve spies returned to the Israelites after spying out the land of Canaan, ten of the men gave so discouraging a report that the hearts of the people filled with fear and they lifted up their voices and cried. They refused to go into the land God had promised them. Later when God gave instructions concerning the warfare necessary to possess the land, He said that the officers of the people were to ask, "Is any man afraid or faint-hearted? Let him go home so that his brothers will not become disheartened too" (Deuteronomy 20:8). It takes spiritual maturity to resist the discouragement of others.

Often our discouragement is a matter of pride. We are discouraged that we are not as good as we thought we were. Either we have seen our own imperfection or it has been pointed out to us. Someone hurt our feelings, or we are lonely. We are disappointed. Arthur Glasser once pointed out to a group of missionary candidates the strategy Satan uses to discourage us. He diagrammed it as downward steps to defeat:

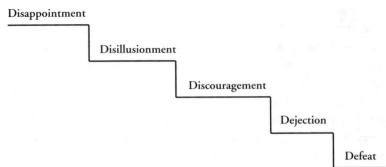

Disappointment

Disillusionment

Discouragement

Dejection

Defeat

If you watch your own emotionally bleak periods you will find this pattern at work. Does one step need to fall into the next? Can we stop the downward pull? Yes, at any point. The remedy is the sacrifice of praise found in Hebrews 13:15, "Let us continually offer to God a sacrifice of praise—the fruit of lips that confess his name."

You may not feel like praising God. That doesn't matter. Do it. Take a psalm of praise and read it until the truth leaps off the page into your heart. Take a hymnal and sing songs of praise. Is God worthy to be praised? Then praise Him; the feeling will come later and His praises will pull you out of the pit.

God lets us cooperate with him in this way, exercising the muscles of our will. The Bible says, "You will keep him in perfect peace whose mind is steadfast, because he trusts in you" (Isaiah 26:3). God's promise is perfect peace, but it is conditioned by our keeping our mind fixed on him. He gave us our will so that we could use it for our good and his praise.

God will not allow us to be passive in experiencing his goodness. The Bible says, "Let your requests be made known to God, and the peace of God, which passes all understanding, will keep your hearts and your minds in Christ Jesus." Our part: let your requests be made known. But the passage goes on: "Whatever is true, whatever is noble, whatever is right, whatever is pure, whatever is lovely, whatever is admirable, if anything is excellent or praiseworthy, think about such things" (Philippians 4:6-8). It's a choice we have to make. Will we be anxious and fuss? Or will we tell Him our requests? Will we allow our minds to dwell on the grubby side of life, or will we furnish our minds with worthy thoughts? Maturity chooses the best in the face of stress.

But anyone who is honest and realistic knows the

downward pull is strong. When life is hard it isn't easy to choose the positive, to focus our minds on God or even to think about other excellent things. We are like Peter walking on the water. We do fairly well, until we begin to look at the waves instead of Jesus. Yet we determine so much about our lives by the exercise of our wills. Elaborate all the psychological bruises that make life grim, and you are still stuck with a grim life. At some point we are left with a decision about our intentionality. What do we intend to do? We may sometimes have our low moments, but God will maximize our intentions.

A maturing Christian realizes that the praiseworthiness of God is the source of all joy. It is His excellence, the steadfastness of His love, the perfection of His character, His faithfulness to mankind that is the wellspring of all joy. Because of Him we can know joy in an imperfect, troubled world. Our feelings of happiness which are dependent on circumstances may come and go. But joy is deep-seated; it is not dependent on circumstances. Jesus said that He wanted His joy to be in us, and that the secret of joy was to abide in Him, as branches abide in the vine (John 15:1-11). Joy comes out of a relationship with God.

From the first announcement of the coming of Jesus Christ into the world, the Scriptures cry out, "Fear not" and "Be of good cheer." God is still God. He intervenes in our human affairs, and He is the source of our encouragement.

Thankfulness characterizes a maturing person. The Bible gives so many instructions about praise and thanksgiving. The New Testament is dotted with the phrase "and be thankful." In Romans 1 when men are described as choosing not to honor God as God, the description of their degeneracy adds, "neither did they give thanks to him." When Paul instructs Christians in Thessalonica about living the Christian life he tells them to "be joyful always, pray continually; give thanks in all circumstances, for this is God's will for you in Christ Jesus" (1 Thessalonians 5:16-18). Thankfulness puts life in perspective. It is a statement that you know you don't deserve all you have; it puts you in a proper relationship with God.

Thankfulness makes people beautiful. It wouldn't hurt us to make a list of things we are thankful for and present it in our prayers before the Lord. Thankfulness lists will vary, but they may include: two bluejays on the branch outside the window, clean sheets, the yawn of a small child, fresh snow, a warm day, cold milk, a warm house, drip-dry clothes, privacy, friendships, the prayers of others. Thankfulness for small things helps us stand in awe of life.

Perhaps the hardest reality to fight through is also our greatest bondage: our need to forgive. Some people carry enormous loads of collected grievances, small hurts and large offenses. Their lives are weighted down until their vision is out of focus. Jesus died so we could lay our load at the foot of the cross. He came to make forgiveness a personal experience for everyone who would trust Him. Since we have been forgiven, He asks us to forgive. No freedom exists apart from our ability to forgive others. Forgiving others is proof that we understand our own forgiveness. If God can forgive me, who am I to fail to forgive someone else?

Among the most beautiful events in human history I have witnessed have been the forgiving events that unite families and friends. Some people have never learned to say, "I'm sorry," and they are usually the ones who cannot say, "I forgive you." Those two phrases put into practice and added to "I love you" are the most freeing experiences in the world.

It takes time to mature, but some have grown old without ever making it. Those who live in this kind of relationship with God grow rich and healthy and beautiful, and those closest to them rise up and call them blessed.

# 7

# THE JOY OF BEING HOSPITABLE

In today's harried world hospitality is almost a lost art. And an art it is! A beautiful, enriching art that demonstrates that giving is better than receiving. The idea is as old as the creation of mankind and comes from the heart of God. God created a hospitable world, but the disorder of selfishness increasingly makes most people feel like strangers in it. One of the saddest verses in the Bible describes the coming of Jesus Christ into the world. "He came to his own home, and his own people received him not" (John 1:11 RSV). God is hospitable; He expects His children to follow His example. "Yet to all who received him, to those who believed in his name, he gave the right to become the children of God."

Hospitality is more than a virtuous deed to be checked off a list; it is a mind-set toward life. The word *hospitable* means receiving guests or strangers warmly and generously; being favorably receptive and open to others. It is letting people into your home and into your life, and its ministry fits our human needs.

Anyone who has experienced this kind of warm reception into a family or a home knows the refreshment it brings the spirit, especially if one is traveling, lonely, or unacquainted in an area. But quite apart from being a stranger or away from home, everyone needs to be wanted and hospitality does that for a person. It says, "You are important to us." No one is too secure or too important not to need these simple gestures of love. Offering hospitality is loving your neighbor as yourself. Many people gladly receive it, but some are reluctant to offer it to others. The very sound of the word may produce the mental image of work, inconvenience, and stress in your mind, but if it does, you are not thinking of hospitality—you are thinking of you.

The Jews had laws defining hospitality, "When an alien lives with you in your land, do not mistreat him. The alien living with you must be treated as one of your native-born. Love him as yourself, for you were aliens in Egypt. I am the Lord your God" (Leviticus 19:33-34). Strangers living with the Israelites the night of the passover in Egypt feasted with the families, according to the rules of circumcision, and were redeemed with Israel.

Think of the rich experience of Abraham entertaining "angels unaware" when the Lord was on His way to destroy Sodom and Gommorah. He saw three men passing by and ran out in oriental fashion and begged them to stay, calling the abundant feast he prepared "a morsel of bread," standing while they ate to show his honor. Such hospitality still exists among nomadic peoples, and many non-Christian cultures have elaborate rituals for the entertainment of guests. In some tribal groups everything the host possesses is given for the use of the guest, including the honor of his wife or daughters. I question that latter generosity! But in such cultures the woman is in the same category as other possessions.

The availability of motels, hotels, and restaurants does not cancel out the need of hospitality as some assume. Rather it places hospitality on a different level and makes its practice less routine and more creative. I think of a friend who, upon meeting a visiting professor from South Africa, immediately arranged for him to come to dinner, inviting others to widen his circle of friendships. After a rented room and cafeteria food, the professor had a whole new feel for our city and our country. What a different kind of entertaining this is than the social obligation routine of going to dinner and then "owing" a dinner in return. The Bible talks about doing good to those who cannot return the favor.

But hospitality is like casting a pebble into a lake. The ripples go to the far shore. We were in Malaysia, attempting to visit the beautiful new air-conditioned government buildings in Kuala Lumpur. Because it was hot outside, the men in our party had neither suit coats nor ties, and both are required for entrance. As we were turning to leave, a tall turbaned Sikh approached us in the friendliest manner and asked if he could help us. He observed we were Americans and said that in his student days in America he had been so cordially received that he determined that whenever he could help an American in his country he would do it. He turned out to be a member of Parliament, and hustled about to borrow ties and suitcoats from clerks working in private rooms. They were ludicrous in fit—size 32 short on a 44 long! But nevertheless, he proceeded to give us a personal tour of the chambers of government. That remains a special memory.

I have often since thought of international students we have entertained who have gone back to similar posts of government, some of them immigration officials who may now determine policies regarding missionary visas. Hospitality is never just the meal or the bed; it is the message you give a person about his value and your own personal values in the gracious giving of what is yours.

### A PERSUADED HEART

In a rural village near our home there was an ill-kempt shoe repair shop run by a strange man whose whole demeanor betrayed the cruel circumstances of his life. He lived with his cats in the back of his shop; his fingernails and the creases in his hands and face were grimy from boot black, coal soot and no hot water; the heavy underwear at the open neck of his shirt showed the neglect of his personal hygiene. He was almost wordless, grunting out replies to his customers. Sometimes he crawled on the floor because he was not wearing the wooden legs he usually hobbled on. I was curious about him and, being new in the village, I asked old-timers about his story. No one I talked with seemed to know. He was just a peculiar man, they said.

But one of our friends, a single man who worked for my husband, moved to this village soon after and, because he possessed a quiet, hospitable spirit, he invited this man into his life. He brought him to his apartment for Thanksgiving dinner, along with a couple of friends who helped him cook his first holiday meal. They ate good food, they talked, they played games, and as the day wore on, our shoemaker began to relax. He could hardly comprehend a place where there was so much love, simple joy, and goodness.

Eventually he told his story. He was an orphan, taken in by a farm family in Canada. He worked hard as a farmhand and more than earned his keep. One bitter cold winter day after he had done the chores, his feet wet and his body numb with cold, he returned to the house only to find the door barred. He had displeased the family and they punished him by locking him out in the cold. He pounded and pleaded to be let in from thirty below zero temperatures. His feet froze; he did not get proper care, and eventually lost his legs.

He had never known love in all his life, until our friend

took him into his life and tried to tell him that God loved him—an almost meaningless concept if you had never experienced human love. A miracle took place because one single man dared to let a needy person into his life.

I mention this example because single people may feel that hospitality means having a family, a house, or proper furnishings. No, it means welcoming the stranger. You can be hospitable in a dormitory room, simply by caring enough to invite someone in so that you can know her and be known by her. The generous use of your car can be creative hospitality; its facets are many.

One of the most beautiful illustrations of hospitality in the Bible is the story of the Good Samaritan. He gave himself to a wounded man who was a stranger. Unable to take him to his own home, he took him to a nearby inn and paid for his care. He was in the middle of the country when he found him, but he did what he could.

The single women I know who have the richest lives are the ones who practice hospitality. They are sensitive to the needs and joys of others and make room in their lives. Given all the varieties in temperament, each woman still has to take inventory: whom have I welcomed into my life? For whom is my leisure time spent? Who are my friends?

The example of hospitality that deeply touches me as I read the Scriptures is the picture of Jesus cooking breakfast for the disciples on the shore of Lake Galilee after His resurrection. Broiled fish on a charcoal fire, and bread. The Lord of glory cooking a meal. He cared about people's needs. I have often thought of Him as I have cooked meals for others.

The book of Acts describes the fellowship of the early church as they broke bread in their homes, partook of food with glad and generous hearts, praising God and having favor with all the people. Imagine what it meant for a new convert to be invited into such a hospitable home—the sharing, the joy, the thanksgiving to God.

The missionary outreach of the church prospered under this kind of hospitality in the first century. In a hostile world, travelers carrying the Good News received the care of other believers. Paul wrote of "Gaius, whose hospitality I . . . enjoy." As the church grew this may have become burdensome at times, for Peter admonishes believers to "offer hospitality to one another without grumbling." Perhaps he needed to say that because a few were doing more than their share.

Hospitality has been part of Christian witness from the beginning. A qualification for the office of bishop is that he must be hospitable (1 Timothy 3:2). Widows who qualify for special ministry in the church must have proven their good works; they must have shown hospitality (1 Timothy 5:10). Hebrew Christians were exhorted, "do not forget to entertain strangers, for by doing so some people have entertained angels without knowing it" (Hebrews 13:2). In Romans 12:13, "practicing hospitality" is one of the traits of the person who has presented his body as a living sacrifice to God. Later in Romans 16:1, Paul asks the Roman Christians to receive Phoebe, a helpful minister from the church at Cenchrea who was coming to Rome. Why is hospitality so important? Because people are so important to God.

Food is an important part of hospitality, and has a way of binding people together. Seated together around the table, the barriers disappear and satisfaction radiates a warm glow. Elaborate or simple, sharing the work of your hands and what you possess refreshes others.

Preparing good tasting food is a way to show people my love, but I have learned not to make the preparation so complicated that I can't enjoy the people. I have a supply of simple, tasty recipes that are neither costly nor laborious. They give me the freedom to say, "Come home for dinner." What is pleasant to look on and good to taste does not so much require labor as developed taste buds, a creative touch—and love. One does not have to be a French chef to know that colors and texture are part of the delight of eating. And a table made pretty with a small bouquet or a candle says, "Come and be with us!"

On a gourmet-cooking program on television the host interviewed a famous personality who commented that she thought it worthwhile to cook well only for a few choice friends because the effort was an expression of love. If she did not care about the people, they went out to a restaurant. She had one thing straight. Good food says, "I care about you," but she was selfish about who she cared for. Some of the people who most need the gracious touch of carefully prepared food are the neglected, unloved ones of this world—the lonely ones who find it hard to feel at home anywhere. My heart has been warmed often by a comment or a note, sometimes received years later, that tells me this kind of hospitality is valuable. I think of one note that read, "You have taught me a lot about the love of God by serving us from your best tea cups and making the table and the food seem so inviting."

But such a ministry is not just for outsiders. Personally I feel I communicate hospitality and love to my own family by the effort of tasty food. In my mind it is the inalienable right of every child to come into the house and smell fresh-baked cookies or bread or something that says, "Yum-m-m. Someone here loves me!" Husbands included, of course. Along with neighbor children, and anyone else who comes in. Homes should have a loving smell.

I am no gourmet cook, but people are welcome at our

table whether they are expected or not. In hospitable homes, the joy of receiving others is catching and becomes a family project. We keep extra cans of food to be opened for unexpected callers. My husband and son both cook a specialty omelet that is hard to beat. Our bean-bacon-cheese sandwiches are winners. And homemade soup from the freezer saves the day on many occasions. Hospitality doesn't mean fancy; it means *I'm glad you are here.* And anyone can help set the table or carry out the dishes!

We know what it means to travel and stay in the homes of others, so we have room "in our inn" for those who need it. I learned long ago to make having guests as easy as possible. Good pillows, enough blankets, a box of tissues, a private drinking glass, and a good light to read by are items I try to provide. When the garden is in bloom I may add flowers on a bedside stand. But we've also let students sleep on the floor wall to wall, and wait in long lines for use of the bathroom. And those have been some of the merriest times.

But hospitality needs to be practiced within the family and within the home as well. It's folly to talk of receiving the stranger when little sensitivity exists within the home to the needs of family members or the apartment mate. Increasingly, families do not eat together, or if they do, their meals are hurried times where everyone is free to gulp down his food and leave the table to watch television. The larger the family, the more difficult it is to make it work, but some time should be sacred in family life when we talk together as a family and get to know what has made up the day of each member. The fellowship of food can also provide the fellowship of sharing. Jimmy does not leave the table as soon as he has finished his food because to do so would be saying that he didn't care about what happened in John's life that day. We stay together and talk. It's a habit, not a punishment.

*The Joy of Being Hospitable*

A question was asked in a small sharing group, "What was the favorite room in your house when you were growing up, and why?" I could immediately answer, "The dinette where we ate our family meals." It was actually an old-fashioned breakfast nook—benches alongside the table with a stool on each end. We had to take our places in the right order and be there on time! But around that table our family members recounted their day, and sometimes my father or mother would have to grant permission to speak in turn because everyone wanted to talk at once. But we grew up knowing each other and caring.

The same principle is true for a single person living with roommates. Mealtimes can be solitary, selfish events, or they can be hospitable times of sharing of food, of getting to know each other, and of demonstrating concern for the other's life.

The pace of life has quickened to the point where our humanity is endangered. We are not pigs at a trough. If we have a quality life, it is because we decided to make it so. Time is not measured so much by quantity as by quality. You can pack much quality into a small amount of time if you determine to do so.

Dr. Graham Blaine, a noted psychiatrist, complains about the use of television in our lives. He says that the most serious problem of TV is not poor programming, but that it has destroyed the average family's conversation at the evening meal. When people are anxious to see a favorite program, they hurry through the meal. He says that what happened during the day, the little things, and bigger matters are never discussed.

Hospitality begins at home.

We have alluded to variety in temperament. There are many variables that affect people's lives: physical stamina, the number of children, ease of motherhood, nature of responsibility, or personality. Some people are gregarious and like people around; others are shy, introverted and prefer privacy. Any one of these factors can be used as an excuse to live a selfish life. Women often paralyze themselves from creativity by comparing themselves with other people. I can't entertain like she does so I won't be hospitable to her. Nonsense. We go to God to find out what He has in mind for our style of showing hospitality, and we do that. When we face our selfishness, our insecurities and our hangups realistically we can act as we should. Hospitality is valuable, not because of style, but because it shows genuine love for others.

One summer years ago we ministered in a small church in a poverty-stricken area where drought ruined the only salable crop almost annually. An older daughter and her father invited us to their home for dinner. They didn't often have company for dinner because the area was sparsely populated and people saved their gas to go to the store and to church. But these people had a warm love for God and they wanted us to come for dinner and talk about Jesus.

I have never felt such an overflow of joy at another's hospitality. Bessie had taken one of her chickens—an egg-layer, thus depleting her source of cash income—and butchered it for our dinner. With those precious eggs she had baked desserts on her wood stove. It was a hot day; the house had no screens and flies swarmed on the food. That hospitality cost Bessie and her dad something, and we have never felt more welcomed. Their happiness in sharing what they had—and the Lord Jesus—will be among our warmest memories forever.

In contrast we have been invited to homes where the obvious effort to have us there had made the whole family uptight. They did not so much want to share themselves as impress us with joyless perfection. I feel that way about fireplaces that are never used to invite someone to sit near them. Joyless cleanliness. And the tragedy often is that the people whose homes are most beautifully appointed often use them the least for others. On what basis do they justify such elaborate possessions?

I have called this chapter *The Joy of Being Hospitable.* Is it really joy? Yes, because hospitality reflects the character of Jesus Christ. It is implicit in the outworkings of the fruit of the Spirit in our lives—love, joy, peace, patience, kindness, goodness, faithfulness, gentleness, and self-control (Galatians 5:22).

*Welcome one another, therefore, as Christ has welcomed you, for the glory of God.* (Romans 15:7 RSV)

# 8

·  ———  ·

# So You're Married

When you said "yes" to Harry, you agreed to "build a nest" or make a home. Many times since then you may have said to yourself, or proclaimed to the world, "But I didn't know it would include this!" What prompted your exclamation could be a moment of sheer bliss or a moment of discontent. You expected only bliss, maybe? Then you forgot that you were still you. You didn't know such bliss existed? Then you are unaware of God's great plan.

The commitment to make a home has such enormous implications that it often takes years to realize how fascinating, how all-encompassing, how strategic your calling really is. But, you may say, I said I'd be a wife, not a homemaker. What you really said may include a far larger assignment than you had in mind, which is precisely why we need solid teaching about the home and the meaning of relationships.

Loving someone in marriage means more than sleeping with them. It is a total commitment of life; it is an overwhelming, lasting desire to give one's self completely to another person and to create for that person an environment in which he or she can become all that God intended him or her to be. It is a building relationship; both partners are happier, stronger, and more fully realized than before their union.

The biblical definition of marriage found in Genesis 2:24 says that a man leaves his father and mother and cleaves to his wife, becoming one flesh with her. Every indication of the strong verbs *leave* and *cleave* point to the establishment of a new home, a new unit. Oneness is the goal. Creating a *home* is a necessity.

Both partners are committed to creating a new thing, something bigger than either of them separately. Their commitment is not just to each other; it is to the new family unit their union has created. In fact, the combined impact of the union of two people from different backgrounds, with different talents, personalities, insights, and character strengths creates something greater than either of them can know at the time. One flesh becomes more rather than less; its sum total is greater than its parts.

Creating the environment, the climate, the quality relationships in which this new union will flourish is part of your job. It is not the wife's job alone, but by the nature of her gifts, which include childbearing and motherhood, she cannot avoid her larger responsibility in this task.

What comes to your mind when you think of the word *home*? If your response is a feeling of safety, of belonging, of love, of acceptance—then you have experienced home, and you have the necessary framework for being a *home* maker. If your reaction to home is one of unhappy memories, quarrels, rejection, and attacks on your personhood, then you will appreciate new dimensions of the importance of home, but you may have to make an even greater commitment to create this positive kind of home because you have not had the right kind of model. I have observed often that those who complain most bitterly about their home background do not make the commitment and effort to change the pattern when they set up their own homes.

Home and family are under attack today. Television sitcoms portray all kinds of off-beat ways for people to live together. With an increasing number of mothers employed in fulltime jobs, children have become involuntary daily commuters to babysitters or nursery schools. The number of latch-key children—those who come home after school to an empty house—is a present-day phenomena. That's only part of the story. Having jobs means having money, and having money means we can opt out of relationships that seem confining. The past two decades have produced more one-parent families than our nation has ever known. Lost people are looking for answers that will help them face commitments they find frightening because they have never experienced them.

Home and family are the basic building blocks in society, and are God's idea. I am increasingly convinced that we ignore their importance to our peril. If people will not commit themselves in the most important relationships in life, is any other commitment valid? The influence of the home outstrips any other in the world. That it should so often be negative in our day says nothing about the vitality of the institution, but a great deal about us.

The home is the most convincing evidence in the world of the reality of the gospel. Here we can see people living in relationship to each other in a way that enhances their personhood, loving each other, solving conflicts, serving one another, and obeying God. But this kind of home doesn't develop by accident or with our left-over efforts; it takes genuine commitment.

Some time ago I was invited to speak to a *Family Living* class at a large university. I went with some trepidation because I didn't know the professor nor the subject matter already covered. It was the early seventies, and I found the usual cross-section of people characteristic of a university: men, women, the carefully unkempt, the anti-establishment costume-wearers, the neatly dressed and well-combed, the open-faced, the reluctant, the friendly, and the sullen. A classroom full of individuals, a motley crew indeed. Why were they enrolled in *Family Living*? Some evidenced studied disinterest as I began; one had his head down on his books, feigning sleep. After some introductory remarks I began to discuss a definition of home. I said, "A home is a safe place. It is a fortress where its members are free from attack. Though each is different, the personhood of each is affirmed..."

I finished the first sentence, and suddenly everyone was at attention, looking at me. *A home is a safe place.* Soft, hungry, wistful looks in those eyes that turned toward me. Something emotional was happening in that classroom, and observing it, I felt a sword of compassion stab my heart. Every single person in that room wanted a safe place! It was written on their faces.

Later I led a discussion on my presentation and I heard remarks like: *I've been looking for a safe place all my life. . . . What makes a home safe? . . . How do you begin?*

It begins with a commitment to build something bigger than yourself—that meets more needs than those of your own small fitfulness. It will take the very best any woman has to offer. It cannot be her casual interest; it must be her major concern. It will drive her to a life with God that is deep and rich and will mean the unconscious expansion of her puny soul. Being a *home* maker is the great adventure God entrusted to a woman, and her influence spreads beyond her imagination.

We live in a merchandising climate today; if a thing

doesn't bring in money, its worth is doubtful. *Home* makers are not paid for their work in dollars, and money is the mark of value in our society. Strong pressure from a variety of quarters makes a young mother doubt whether it really is making good use of her education to stay at home tending a two-year-old and a new baby. "I have a master's degree that is just going to waste." If our idea of education is so utilitarian, I doubt if we have any appreciation of its value. Since when is education only designed to bring in money? I thought it was to provide some inner wealth in terms of being.

I stand up in this age of uncertain values and proclaim a mother's right not to have to work outside the home. Being a *home* maker is no small task when children are involved. Women are finding this out. Trying to carry on two equal careers is a frustrating and exhausting task, even if she has a mate who shares the load. Increasing numbers of women are opting for "cottage industry" or work that can be done at home in an attempt to avoid the financial crunch of child-care, as well as absence from their children.

Not everyone has the luxury of choice. The single mothers who are called to do double duty need the support and help of friends who care. How happily most of these would give up dual responsibility if they could! For other women, working is considered a necessity to make ends meet in the family budget. The decision to let others raise your children is a tough one. It calls for a tight, wise value judgment that should be reviewed often.

While working mothers were once a rarity, today the mothers who stay at home with their children are becoming the minority group. My niece has chosen that path, but finds that at social gatherings people who ask her, "What do you do?" hardly know how to respond when she says that she is a *home* maker. She doesn't use the old routine of "I'm just a housewife," but people assume that someone who stays at home isn't very interesting. I suggested she answer, "Jim and I have decided to raise our own children!" and see if that gets the same response.

Working is not the issue; our motivation and sense of purpose is. It has almost become a new gospel: If you want to be fulfilled and have your dreams realized, get outside employment. And with women making up half of the nation's labor force, the working wife is a fact of life. However, it is not meaningless to ask the question: Does my present lifestyle enable me to make the largest contribution to the good of my children, my spouse, and myself?

I regard the profession of a *home* maker too highly not to sound a warning lest a great calling go unappreciated—a calling which profoundly affects our society.

I know all about the mothers who are frustrated career women—who live vicariously through their children. I know about the club women, the over-volunteered who neglect their home, seeking fulfillment apart from a job. There are many ways to be self-centered. You can prove almost anything from a survey if you word the questions right, and if you ask the right people. Only recently I read a survey that claimed that the role of wife and mother meant sacrificing self-esteem, a deficiency that showed up in middle age, while the career woman had a growing sense of self-worth. Married career women viewed themselves as better mothers and more attractive to men than non-working wives, which proves exactly nothing. The process is called rationalization.

Choosing up sides and voting on the right-to-work doesn't give us the answer. We need God's perspective on a larger commitment and His personal direction for our lives. He judges our motives, and it is here that we stand and fall. If our goal is simply the luxury of two incomes, wanting to feel important (instead of being important to a few) or having to prove our worth—God has some more basic, eternally satisfying ways to meet those needs.

Our problem is not so much one of lost identity, but lost goals. And the lost goals are evidenced in divorce rates, in delinquent, confused children, and in our shallow, meaningless lives. We need to conduct our lives on the basis of reality, not on the data found in magazine articles or surveys.

A married woman's first duty is to know her husband. Every marriage is a unique combination of two personalities. We might need to add of two people who are sinners because sometimes the blinding glare of love leads us to believe that *eros* has transported us beyond our faults. Given all the differences that exist between two people, that oneness of purpose and action can occur in a marriage is proof of the grace of God. But it is so often the little foxes that spoil the vines: he doesn't hang up his clothes; he leaves the washcloth in the sink; he doesn't wipe his feet. Oh, for the wisdom to know the difference between what is important and what is trivial. Every woman needs to learn how to distill the sweetness from the mixture of every day's experiences. Otherwise her attention to detail can become so perverted that she may consider her husband the enemy of her household—which scarcely qualifies as making a *home* for someone. Some women are more in love with neatness than with their husbands.

Knowing a person is the adventure of marriage. Partners rarely come together with highly developed skills in self-disclosure. Knowing your husband means observing his habits, his likes, and dislikes—but it goes beyond that. What makes him uptight and what comforts him? How does he think and what does he feel? Notice that the list moves from the less complicated to the greater understanding. If we fail in comprehending and ministering in the area of the simple, what are our chances for success in the complex? For instance, granted that a man can learn how to hang up his pajamas, a wife can make such a big deal out of this that she closes him off from any deeper level of communication.

Individuals are programmed differently. I'm a turnip in the morning. I roll up into a ball and want to stay underground for a while. In contrast, my husband wakes with a song. Every day is beautiful for him and he moves with vigor into it. If he takes more than eight deep breaths at night before falling asleep, he thinks he has insomnia. More often than not, I lie and re-do my day before falling asleep. When I was a new bride (he has managed to make me feel like a bride for years) I sometimes woke him up because I felt he had deserted me and I was lonely. We laugh about that now because it resembles a television commercial.

But his habits have been good for me. I've come to love his cheery whistle coming from the bathroom while I shake myself out of my drowsiness. And he has long since given up the idea that I will bound out of bed first, if indeed he ever expected it. I know he likes a good breakfast, and he wants to begin the day with everyone around the table. And so this is what we do at our house, and as I listen to him read the Scripture and pray for the details of the day each one faces, I'm grateful he had the warm, good sense to insist on living this way.

But another husband may be the opposite. He may not want to speak until twenty minutes after his first cup of coffee. You may want to discuss all the things you forgot the night before over breakfast. Adjustments are necessary for both people in a marriage, and they come with knowing each other, talking about living together, and a decision not to bump into a person where they already hurt. And hurts do heal and living patterns do change. That's what growth is all about.

I remember hearing a story of a man speaking to his wife on his deathbed. He said, "Honey, just before I go I want to tell you one thing. I really haven't minded eating all those chicken livers you gave me ever since we were married, even though I hate chicken livers."

"Oh, dear," she said, "and all these years I have watched you eating them and wished I could have them!"

That's a slap-stick illustration of poor communication. God gave us speech so we could talk, and most marriages need help on the level of better communication. Never be content with low quality in this area. A creative God wants to draw us out of our aloneness into the joy of fellowship. But some women are guilty of over-kill with their verbal skills. It's called nagging. And it does kill husbands; it kills their desire to communicate.

"A little more carrot and a little less stick" is an old proverb for getting along with donkeys. And while not wanting to put husbands and donkeys in the same league, it is a principle of life for *home* makers. Husbands thrive on love; so do children. The creative *home* maker finds many ways to scatter love around in her life, and finds its rich dividends returning to her.

The Bible uses the marriage relationship to illustrate the relationship God has with His people. Israel is called the wife of God in the Old Testament, in the New Testament the church is called the bride of Christ. These analogies profoundly instruct us in our Christian life and in our married life. For example, imagine Christ abusing the church or being unfaithful to her. Or the church refusing or accusing

Christ. The quality of earthly relationship is elevated by the mystery of our quality relationship with the living God.

But perhaps the most familiar biblical passage about marriage is also the least understood. Paul gives instructions about relationships in his letter to the Ephesian church. His theme is the unity found in Christ. He instructs Christians in practical relationships between husbands, wives, children, parents, employees, and employers. He begins by teaching that all Christians should be submissive to one another (Ephesians 5:21); that is, they should receive encouragement, exhortation, rebuke, and instruction from one another because this kind of humility marks those who belong to the Christian family.

Then he goes on to give the instructions read at almost every church wedding ceremony: "Wives, submit to your husbands, as to the Lord. For the husband is the head of the wife as Christ is the head of the church, his body, of which he is the Savior. Now as the church submits to Christ, so also wives should submit to their husbands in everything" (Ephesians 5:22-24). With an angry glint in the eye, many women have accused Paul of perpetrating his prejudices. If their presupposition about marriage is based on togetherness, not oneness, they may have virtually no comprehension of the context of the instruction nor the ideal behind it.

The instruction does not necessarily mean that the husband has superior intelligence, wisdom, or ability; it simply means he is responsible to God for the family. This being so, God's instructions (and I believe they are God's instructions given through Paul) are that wives should be submissive to their husbands, as to the Lord. In other words, make it easy for your husband to become what God wants him to be. Just because he is a man doesn't mean he is naturally buoyant with self-confidence. Don't destroy his leadership. Hold him to his highest. Your submission says nothing about inferiority or superiority, just as his being "head" is no comment on his. It is simply fulfilling responsibility.

The instruction to wives doesn't seem to have a loophole. The text does not say "be submissive *if* he loves you as Christ loves the church." It says be submissive in everything as to the Lord. Submission is a Christian idea. The opposite of submission in relationships is probably arrogance. Christ demonstrated the finest kind of submission. He willingly washed His disciples' feet; He willingly submitted Himself to the cross. Submission does not mean that you never have an opinion, a complaint, or an original idea. Some men have used this instruction as a put-down for their wives, keeping them uninformed about important family affairs and acting as if their wives were mentally incompetent. That is not even implied in this passage because of its emphasis on oneness. God holds such men responsible for egotistic, domineering leadership which does not reflect His own character. The instruction for the husband to love his wife as Christ loved the church—sacrificially (He died for her), purposefully (He has a high goal in mind for her), and willfully (His love knows no whims)—precludes this kind of behavior.

But that is the husband's problem, not the wife's. The wife's problem may be that she is often willful and competitive, so aggressive and verbal that the husband abdicates his leadership, believing the wife can run the home and family better anyway. And no wife is really happy with that arrangement. A happy marriage experiences a mutuality, an enhancing, a oneness that reflects the character of God.

The verbal skills of some women may intimidate men and cause them to clam up. That becomes both the man and the woman's problem to solve together. He needs to be less threatened and carry on with leadership under God. She needs to be more cautious in her speech. But articulation does not equal leadership, as some assume. Character strength and personal integrity are the real tests of leadership.

Good leaders are not dictators. A man's wife is often his best consultant, and the reverse is true as well. In that sense a man and a woman make decisions together. Hierarchy in leadership should not surprise us; it is seen in most human enterprises. It exists within the Godhead. Jesus said He always did the will of His Father in heaven, and was subject to Him. Did this diminish Christ in any way? I think not.

The whole discussion of relationships in Ephesians 5 and 6 is vitally important because high goals undergird all the instructions. They are not meaningless, rigid laws designed to make our life hard. God has a high goal in mind for wives, for husbands, and for children.

Too few married people sit down and talk about adequate goals for their marriage. Without some concept of goals, the home can become a battleground where each grabs to fill personal needs, abusing the other. No woman who is consumed with filling her own emptiness and inner need can make a *home* for anyone else. She's too immature. Her myopia keeps her from seeing beyond her own needs.

Often in the battles of such a household one person is exploited by the other and becomes a shell instead of a person. Sometimes a husband rules the roost with cocksure opinions, relegating his wife to the servitude of providing for his needs, negating her person. And just as frequently, the wife becomes the domineering, possessive one, relegating her husband (and her children) to opinionless existence. Whatever the case, such marriages reduce the strength of both persons below their separate strengths.

Another kind of marriage may equal the separate strength

of both the man and the woman. Each pursues a separate goal, going his individual way. Two people live together in the same house, but are not involved in each other's life in any way which changes the individual's potential. The partners remain free agents, each pursuing his own course. I believe this falls short of the biblical ideal, and confines each person to the prison of self.

The one-flesh concept soars off to greater heights than this. Both husband and wife work toward goals they set for themselves as a unit. Each is more fully realized as they operate as an entity. They are building something bigger than themselves, involving the will of God for their life together. Both husband and wife are liberated in this kind of marriage.

Children who are born into this kind of home are already enrolled in a head-start program. They are less likely to become pawns in the play-off between husband and wife, because everyone is playing on the same team. And there is a game plan. The family has already decided what is valuable, what is worthwhile, and which road to take.

Being a *home* maker for children is the second delight of a woman. Their whole view of life will be conditioned by your creativity in this role. Their view of God, of safety, of forgiveness, of love, of loyalty—and thousands of other attitudes will come from you and your husband. By sheer virtue of the close relationship necessitated by care, you will influence them most. You will furnish their spirits with the concepts out of which they will build their lives.

After cleaning up a mess for the fifth time in one day, it is a rare young mother responsible for a couple of preschoolers who does not feel like abandoning everyone and going off on a Caribbean cruise. And she doesn't have to pretend she doesn't feel that way. Her husband, in the pressure-cooker of his job, may wish he could escape having to earn a living and run away to climb the Alps too. That's the stuff life is made of, and our commitment to a quality life provides the ballast to keep the ship on course.

To bear and rear children is to take on both joy and sorrow, but this is the heart of living. To present to the world and to the church a covey of people who know how to live and who are not threatened by the world is a gift to humanity beyond comparison.

But the danger for the *home* maker is that she will lose her sense of humor and begin to take on super-mother qualities in her zeal to do a good job. Self-consciousness can make us try too hard and we can mutilate both our marriage and our children. Probably the biggest boon to raising children is our own mental and spiritual health. We need to learn that fussing doesn't do as much as praying, that consistency is a gem of rare beauty, that discipline and allowing appropriate independence are part of growing up. Loving will mean standing with one foot in the child's life and one foot in the realities of a hard world, for the person who loses the child inside her is in no shape to teach anyone about the world.

A *home* maker realizes that she is making the *home* for people, not for pages in a magazine. The compulsive housekeeper has to remember that perfection is not the goal; wholeness and a comfortable sense of well-being come first. Nothing can kill her joy more quickly than jealousy over what someone else has. How can they afford that? has spoiled the splendor of many obvious personal blessings.

But, having said that, a child deserves to grow up in an atmosphere of beauty. And he needs to learn that everything in life is not for his use. Be such an atmosphere ever so simple and inexpensive, the *home* maker has the freedom to create this kind of environment. A vase of forsythia being forced to bloom in early March, a candle on a low table, flowers on a sick tray, pictures rightly arranged, a place for things that seems just right. Things to admire, things not to touch, things that make the room seem cozy and warm. In my mind, being a *home* maker can be the most creative job in the world, and I have great admiration for young mothers I know who surround those they love with a charm that was first born in the heart of Eve.

Phillips Brooks said, "Duty makes us do things well, but love makes us do them beautifully."

A woman can grow beautiful and strong being a *home* maker. Potentially the position can bring out the best in her because it will tax and test all her resources. But it can also provide the opportunity for her to grow small and petty. It's like any other job in that respect. A woman can regard her children as possessions and harry them to distraction with her demand for perfection or performance that matches the neighbor's children. Her obsession with her house can make her a complaining nuisance. Her jealousy of her husband and her unwise intervention can create a continual feud. She may be so involved with the children that she neglects her husband completely. She can grow unaware of the trials and temptations of his life, and fail to hold him to the commitment of their common goals.

If she compares herself with others, she is bound to suffer defeat. She has to like herself and believe in her natural abilities to do the job. She may not be clever in one area, but she can excel in another. Elsewhere in the world, people take differences in natural ability for granted. Somehow within the home, the woman often believes she has to be a super-person. Personalities differ, so does natural wisdom. The size of the family alone makes demands on a woman, and some women find motherhood easier than others. Success comes in different-shaped packages to those who accept themselves and are wise enough to hang on to the resources of God.

Part of the stress on a woman's life derives from her constantly changing role. First she is a bride, learning the basics of relating to her husband; then she is the mother of small children who need much attention; in the next phase she finds herself involved in lessons, in baking cookies for a school party, in transportation; then suddenly she doesn't feel as needed as she once did and she struggles over her children's independence. She may even make the mistake of believing she is no longer needed and become too busy to observe and listen, losing communication with her children at a crucial point in life. Time goes on through a series of phases, and suddenly the nest is empty and she is back to the days of being a bride. Happy is the woman who has managed to stay a bride, a lover, through the years. And happy too is the woman who has managed to maintain her own sense of personhood during all the years when she gave herself so generously to others.

Seeing the stress and the changes in a woman's life, some opt for an easier course, trying to beat off the hazards. But hazards are numerous on other roads too, and the joys are fewer.

I came across a prayer that seems appropriate for *home* makers.

*Lord, teach us to be twice as tough*
*and twice as tender as only*
*the truly tough can be tender.*

# 9

# A WORM IN THE APPLE

Life for the single woman has never looked better. Professionally she can enter almost any field her abilities and inner drive might inspire. The career woman is definitely a positive concept in today's world. She often owns her own car, has her own house, and has the freedom to order her life without having to take others into account. An aura, a mystique hovers over her.

But that's only half the story. The single woman must still battle the instinct of her heart and body, the injustice of discrimination, and sometimes even a feminist raid on her value system. If she is restless, there is irony in her discontent. There aren't enough men to go around: 105 women to every 100 men. And some of the women who have the men seem strangely unhappy with the idea of belonging to them. They complain of having lost their identity, while it may seem to the unmarried women that society is structured to give identity only to the married. There's a worm in the apple no matter where you bite!

"Little girls want to be princesses, but little boys don't want to be princes," writes Sydney Harris, "and from those two different starting points come all the confusions, contradictions, and cross-purposes of courtship and marriage." And we might add—nonmarriage.

Many single women have to wrestle repeatedly with the longing to be married. Loneliness is very real. It is hardly an issue one settles once for all. A woman generally has a stronger sense of the need for a personal bond than a man, and linking her life with the right man makes sense to a woman. Observing this, some have categorized women as dependent, which is not necessarily so. Dependency has different connotations than the innate desire to be part of someone else. A desire to give herself is part of a woman's genetic make-up.

Handling this inner longing presents a problem to the single woman. She may often feel frustrated and even angry at God. She may feel deprived of sex and motherhood. She may not be sufficiently career-oriented to find natural satisfaction in other roles. She resents a society where males have the privilege of initiative, and females must wait to be asked. But she has to feign contentment. If she allows her disappointment at being unmarried to show, she is the brunt of jokes and ridicule. Others sympathize if she sorrows over a lost love, but if no dashing cavalier, whether bold, fat, or handsome, has ever appeared on the scene she must carry on as if she didn't care. In fact, the church often asks her to be super-human about her disappointment.

Fortunately, the road has turned so that open, honest admissions are easier and the world offers a variety of opportunities and personal fulfillments. The single woman looks around and cannot help seeing a disproportionate number of restless, frustrated married women. If she is wise, she probably will question what does make a woman happy anyway. It is true that we tend to be dreamers, however. We often envy the privileges of others and are sure we would never have their difficulties. The single woman who wants to marry is not comforted by the failures of others. We take only positive examples when we make our comparisons and complaints. That's human optimism, and it's a good thing. Offering consolation to a single woman by suggesting that at least she's avoiding the unhappiness of some marriages may only show you don't understand her predicament.

Somewhere along the line women ought to catch on that marriage does not automatically equal happiness. But it may still seem like a pleasant out from a world where personal female value is computed by the relationship a woman has to a man. Failure for a woman in some circles is not to be chosen by a man.

The 1970s ushered in a different tone for male/female relationships. With more career options open and more respect in the marketplace, women are working alongside men in a new camaraderie. And many are delaying marriage. Whether from fear of commitment, or wanting to keep their options open as long as possible, most single women today have mainstreamed in the career track.

It doesn't matter which a woman chooses—happy in career or longing for marriage—her self-view is critical. The only relationship that defines our worth is the one we have with God. Every woman should have the chance to be her unique self without the trappings and trimmings of psychological hangups or society's pressures. She not only has the right to be an individual, she has the obligation to be one. She cannot make any useful contribution to life unless she does. After all, the purpose of life is to live it eagerly and without fear. The single woman may long to be able to sign her name "Mrs. Ted Jones," while the married woman fusses about having no identity other than "Ted's wife" or "Sara's mother." Both positions are ridiculous. It reminds me of a song, you only want it 'cause you haven't got it.

When the Bible refers to women it usually speaks about married women. This is a societal norm. But can you take phrases which refer to married women and paste them on unmarried women? For instance, in Genesis when God speaks to Eve about her future, he says, "Your desire will be for your husband and he will rule over you." What does this say to the single woman? Does it say that a single woman should let men "rule over her"? In Ephesians 5:22 and 1 Corinthians 11:3, wives are to be submissive to their husbands, the husband being the head of the relationship. While a general principle of the leadership of man exists throughout Scripture there seems little basis for saying that all women must be submissive to all men. Rather both men and women are urged to be submissive to one another (Ephesians 5:21), thus displaying the Christian graces of humility and love and reflecting their common submission to Jesus Christ. Submission comes out of relationship.

I think it is safe to say that women want leadership from men, and part of their rebellion comes at the failure of men to act responsibly. Many a dominant, nagging wife is secretly crying out for the man to do what he ought to do. But leadership is different than lording it over the woman. Paul says that the whole plan is God's idea; male and female share dependent relationships (1 Corinthians 11:11-12).

Women are exploited emotionally about physical beauty. Badgered by Madison Avenue's manipulation of a natural desire to be attractive, many women go through painful anxieties over their appearance. And that's not all bad. Every woman ought to look as good as she can. Sloppiness is no virtue; neither is a head of hair that needs a good styling job. Perfume smells better than body odor. Too many rolls of fat are neither healthy nor pretty; and a scrubbed-looking face is more pleasant than an overly-painted one. Looking our best makes us stand taller and gives us more confidence.

Our mistake comes when we derive our value from our physical appearance. If we believe that an unattractive nose makes an unattractive person, we've lost the battle at the first pass. In respect to ourselves, we must not be found hating thick ankles more than an ugly soul!

More important than beauty is the reputation of your person. What words do people use to describe you? What words would you like them to use? The discrepancy in your answers may indicate what your priorities should be.

All women are potentially selfish simply because they are human. The hazards for single women to become rigid and self-centered are greater. The married woman will have her selfishness contested by both her husband and her children. If she doesn't outgrow it, she leaves a scar on more than one life. The disaster for the single person comes when she retreats from inter-personal relationships and increasingly grows inflexible, opinionated, set in her ways, and miserably self-centered.

Some women are neurotic; they may need to change either their job or their outside interests. Others have sharp, shrill voices; they need to relax inside and learn how to laugh and play. Some women come into any friend's life like a two-ton Mack truck; they need to examine what dominance-need makes them act this way. Some women have trouble loving, and need to learn the freedom love brings.

But many women grow older and single with quiet good humor and rich lives. They spread love and light and joy around because they have a large supply of it inside. They enter the lives of others with an easy grace. They are interesting, loving human beings who aren't obsessed with their singleness. Men like them; so do women. Usually they have a high calling and are doing what they enjoy.

These women have not let singleness define life for them. They are confident of their personal worth and live with a wholesome awareness and aliveness to the world that belies any stereotyped image. No one pities them because their lives are wide and full and rich.

In fact, the kind of single women I am thinking about could rightly be called sensuous. Sensuous is a word that needs to be rescued from purely sexual connotations. To be sensuous means to be present in every moment of life—feeling life, enjoying it, learning, exploring, appreciating the world God made and the people in it. It is simply to be alive in one's senses.

Many of these women have given themselves to large purposes in life. They may feel called by God not to marry to fulfill the task, to use the gift, to finish the job. In short, they are caught up in an adventure larger than their own life, and in the end this is what makes life significant and fulfilling for anyone.

In particular, women have done an incredible job in the mission of the church with an enthusiasm and a dedication that puts men to shame. Women counselors, teachers, doctors, nurses, translation specialists, writers—the list of noble achievements is known only to God. The important factor for us to observe is that these women have linked their life with God and the ultimate meaning of the universe. Anyone who looks at such a woman and bemoans, "What a pity she didn't marry!" has a small view of what living is all about. From my point of view, I'd rather ask a question about the judgment of the men who passed up these noble women to choose an often shallow, self-centered woman instead. But I am content to let God be the

Sovereign who calls such women into adventure with Himself.

Some women decide that they do not want to marry and settle into a single life. They do not live with either the joy or sorrow of expectancy. Others take matters into their own hands and maneuver for marriage, sometimes with a panic that lacks the dignity of personhood. Whichever the case, such women can cut themselves off from the surprises of God. The "resigned" woman, whether married or single, lacks the vibrancy that expectation brings. And if a woman knows a creative God she may be in for all sorts of surprises.

Why do you want to marry? is an important question. Marrying for the wrong reasons has brought all the miseries the single woman can't avoid noticing. Grabbing at marriage to fill inner emptiness soon reveals that marriage is a false god. Marriage does not change one's essential character or nature. Nor is it a happiness button. A second question, Are you becoming the person the kind of man you want would marry? We keep wanting to conjugate the verbs *to find, to want, to do,* forgetting that the most important verb is *to be.* What you are becoming is vitally important.

Reasons for marriage usually fall in the category labeled human or emotional or physical. Safety, protection, companionship, provision, sex, status—the list could go on. But the list is only valid for a Christian when the larger spiritual factor is taken into consideration: Is this marriage the will of God? And the will of God lines up with the principles of marriage found in the Scriptures.

Which brings us to the point of the goodness of God. God's will is never second best; His will is always first best! To define for God the only way you can be happy is to say you don't really believe in either His goodness or His love. And when life isn't going according to our dreams, it's easy to ask,

"How can a good God do this?" The Bible assures us that He calls each of us by name; all the "walls" of our lives are clearly known to Him. The first step to real life is always hooked up to our relationship with God. If we do not believe we are loved by Him we can go on an endless search for love. It is not idle, easy talk to say that our most profound contentment is found in Christ.

If she fails to believe in the goodness and love of God, strange things can happen to a woman. She grows brittle inside. Blaming external circumstance for lack of fulfillment or frustration, she uses the cutting edge of sarcasm to make her way through life. Or she becomes uptight, a kind of pseudo woman, domineering and brusque. Harboring resentments, making mountains out of mole hills, she throws her failures on someone else. She begins to live against the world. It's the dread disease of dissatisfied womanhood.

Every woman has to work through her own set of barriers. She cannot do this as long as she refuses to face reality. A woman's challenge is to make a success either of one's celibacy or one's marriage. Both require effort, commitment, and development of inner resources. If a woman spends her time dreaming only of what could be or living in an unreal existence, she ceases to live in the now. And no one is attracted to an empty shell. You don't start living when a man comes into your life; you have to live now. You have to be someone worth knowing whether married or single, if life is to be rich.

But what about sex? you ask. Every magazine you pick up features either articles or advertisements for books or products elaborating the importance of the sexual experience. Never has history known such diligent struggle over the orgasm. It's like a strange cult. Everything you've ever wanted to know or experience studied in a laboratory. Sex becomes the summum bonum of life. And I've heard women say, "It would be terrible to die never having known a man sexually." And some have sold their souls for a cheap experience. The woman's right to an orgasm has become a tenet of militant feminism.

We do have a sex drive. Admit it. You can talk to God about it, since He gave it to you. Sexual desire is real. But no one has died yet from perpetual virginity, and sublimation does not scar the psyche. Sex is not a basic human need; love is.

Mental and physical health demand that we act wholesomely on this point and refuse to buy the world's point of view. This may mean that upon awaking we refuse to lie in bed thinking sleepy, erotic thoughts. We learn how to discipline our thought life and we plan a program of physical exercise to work off some steam, just as men do who make a commitment to chastity.

Because of propaganda that overestimates the worth of the sexual experience as a thing in itself, some women have fallen into the trap of masturbation. Affluence provides privacy, and for those looking for a phony thrill, the magazines even offer manipulators for sale. The woman who thus involves herself in self-love digs a pit for herself that only has a miry bottom. Increasingly normal relationships lose their value and a sickness of self-absorption destroys one's self-respect. It's the devil's lie because it says that God is cheating you from what you need; you have to supply your own needs. Playing dumb is no feminine virtue; neither is playing with yourself or exploiting some other female in the game called lesbianism. Beware of propaganda that suggests worship at the wrong shrine. The wise woman looks beyond momentary satisfaction to ask "What will I be like at 65?"

Never be content with trivia. You can squeeze your heart dry over nothing. The attitude of faith is the only truly human one because it gets us beyond ourselves and focuses our attention on the purpose in the universe. We can be conscious of doubts, but we need to be more conscious of God. We need to get our approval, our sense of being loved and worthwhile from Him, not from the response of those around us.

A fearful spirit plagues some women and keeps them from trying anything new. I've tried skiing and as soon as I think I'm going to fall, I fall. It's like the verse in Proverbs 22:13 where the sluggard says, "There is a lion outside! I shall be slain in the streets!" Stay inside. Wait, don't live.

In the final analysis, whether a woman is married or single, she has two choices: either to live her life reluctantly or with conviction. If she lives it with conviction she will find an outlet in life, a way to use her energy, her love, her gifts, her mind—her totality—in a way that will bring deep fulfillment. A single woman who thinks marriage is the only worthwhile adventure is going to have a shriveled life. She needs to like what she is doing now. And with all the choices in the world and given a creative God, it isn't likely that a person cannot find a niche in life that already has her name on it. It may be a growing niche, but she won't find it if she lives like a butterfly, flitting from place to place, unwilling to commit herself to the discipline of self-discovery.

For some this will be working in partnership with or assisting a worthy man, making a contribution to his work, enjoying his friendship and the camaraderie of work. For others it will be soaring to new heights on your own. Since femininity is enhanced by masculinity, the intellectual and social exchange with men is a desirable part of life, and it falls in the realm of meaningful friendships which enhance our lives. I think single women can realistically pray for these kinds of male friendships. The quickest way not to realize them is to communicate that you have more in mind than friendship.

No substitute for godliness exists for any woman. God has in mind an abundant life for every believer. If we are not growing it is because we have not handled what God has told us to handle. We can complain about our lot in life and fuss over our lack of understanding and be much like Job. He was only comforted when God showed him who He was. An adequate view of God takes care of lots of foolishness. His command in our lives is permission, not repression. He makes us free to do that which prepares us for joy—that which will bring the greatest happiness to us.

# 10

## SILVER BELLS AND COCKLE SHELLS

How does your garden grow? For years you've been planting ideas, dreams, deeds, and attitudes in the soil of your life. The fragrance and fruit of your plantings are now affecting others. I'm talking about your ministry—the nourishment your life gives someone else. Ministry is the expression of what is inside you; it is the outflow of what you are.

Technically, *ministry* means to serve, help, or comfort on behalf of someone else. In Britain the word is used of government agencies designed to help people; for example, the Ministry of Education. Educational aid is given on behalf of the government. When we use the word *ministry* in a Christian sense, we carry this same idea. Service, encouragement, comfort given on behalf of someone else, and that Someone is God. Unfortunately, *ministry* has become a professional, clerical word meant only for those on the payroll of the church. Rather it is meant to be the overflow of the life of God in a person.

Ministry implies the importance of people. Jesus said that whenever someone gives a cup of water to a thirsty person, feeds the hungry, or clothes the naked, it is the same as if it were done to Him. That's how important people are to God. When David finally confessed his sin with Bathsheba to God, he said his sin had been against God. Why? Not just because David had broken the law, but the law was there in the first place because God made Bathsheba, and her personhood was important to Him. The entire Bible spells out the importance of people in God's sight. The two great commandments tell us to love God with our whole being, and our neighbor as our self. When God fills a life with Himself, ministry is a natural fruit.

Let's take a look at your ministry. You may be one of those people who think of ministry in terms of a stirring talk, a magnificent prayer or a beautiful song. A public performance means ministry to you and you say, "I have no ministry." If you really have no ministry, it is not for lack of a talent but because of inner barrenness. The influence of a growing, aware life with God will always be more profound than you know. You may not be shouting, "Look at me ministering" but that's just as well. That kind of ministering leads to pride. It's like having too much sun in your garden; it dries out the roots.

I've always liked Barnabas, whom I met in the book of Acts. His chief ministry seemed to be that of encouraging other people. When others were wary of a converted Paul, Barnabas found him and encouraged him to exercise his ministry. Paul became the outstanding missionary, but Barnabas' encouragement got him going. Later when Paul was disappointed with the instability of John Mark, it was Barnabas who took John Mark as his companion and encouraged him in the ministry.

Encouragement is a spiritual ministry; it is God's ministry to you. He always encourages you. If you feel discouraged, you'll find Satan is the source of discouragement. Check out your own garden. Is encouragement one of the strong plants in your life? Encouragement brings out the best in people; it is love taking hold of another hand and placing it in the courage of God.

Everyone can share in this ministry. It takes various forms—understanding, listening, sowing seeds of praise, praying, sharing a godly perspective, or simply saying, "I'm sticking with you." I don't mean Pollyanna-sunshine talk that doesn't face a real world. Encouragement is the overflow of the life of God in you.

Sometimes I think a mother has almost a fulltime ministry of encouragement. My mother set the tone for our whole day by her attitude toward us as we awoke each morning. She often had a song, and always a word of good cheer. The critical, nagging mother can effectively ruin a whole day before it begins. It takes a good portion of creativity to encourage children to be their very best. It's a tough world out there, as you already know.

Hashing over past naughtiness and spouting out negative expectations produces naughtiness and negative behavior. You get what you expect. Encouragement, on the other hand, can help a child to believe in himself and in God.

And what of encouraging your parents as they grow older or your fellow teacher or the neighbor in the next apartment? Anyone who herself is encouraged by God can encourage others. That's the secret. In the Old Testament when David was beset by danger from King Saul, the Scripture reads, "David found strength [encouragement] in the Lord his God" (1 Samuel 30:6). Then David was in a position to encourage others.

The mother in the grocery store, chastising and humiliating her child with loud, angry words that have a far more lasting sting than a spanking, demonstrates the life that has no inflow of divine resources. She lives an uptight life, and probably has many complaints to share with her husband and friends. But who encourages her? What a difference a positive word could make in her life. Encouragement has a ripple effect, flowing out to others. Encouragement! What a magnificent fragrance comes from you. Lord, sow such seeds liberally in our lives.

I have a beautiful friend with five small children. She is sensitive to each child's needs in an unusual way and tries to encourage each one where they need it. And her spirit is catching. I notice that the children encourage each other because of her encouragement. They were all at the school program together one night to watch David perform. He goofed and missed his cue, and the whole family suffered with him, knowing how much it meant to him to do well. Afterward, I heard them as they gathered around David, who bemoaned his error. One sympathized, another mentioned how clearly he spoke his lines—each one thought of something encouraging to say to comfort David, because he was so important to his family.

Anyone who wants a worldwide ministry needs only to learn to pray. Prayer unleashes the activity of God on behalf of those brought before Him—and it changes us. It is the most enriching of ministries because it brings us into God's presence. We become like the people with whom we spend time. But prayer is the most neglected of ministries. Too often our humanness wants our ministry to be seen by others. We need visible, immediate response. No one knows how much we pray, except God. Jesus told us to pray in secret, but assured us that our heavenly Father sees in secret. And He gives His rewards.

Too many of us would rather fuss and feel sorry for ourselves than pray. Prayer can keep a husband on track, realizing the best for his personal life. Prayer can take away a mother's bitterness, can change a father's drunkenness, can alter situations and attitudes, can keep children safe in a strife-filled school. Job prayed for his children, lest they be careless in sinning. Hannah prayed for a godly son. You can pray for a calm heart, a gentle spirit, and for all the sensitive miracles needed in the dynamics of your life.

The King James Version of the Bible uses the word *succour* when it speaks of the help God offers in time of need. It means adequate, appropriate help. I was reading Hebrews 2 one day in my quiet time and I began questioning what kind of help God would offer. What would the quality of His help be? It came to me forcefully that He would offer only holy help. It would be consistent with His character. Then I saw why I didn't always go to Him for the help I needed. If the help offered was holy then I would have to change. That meant self-pity had to go, attitudes would have to be changed. Praying invites God to change our situation—and us.

And you can pray beyond your walls. Years ago we were asked to call on a sick woman from our church. We visited her, hoping to give encouragement, and came away twice blessed. The woman was old, bed-ridden, and childless. Her husband in his own feebleness took loving care of her. Essentially both of them were cut off from active participation in the world. Yet next to her bed the husband had devised a pyramid stand that turned on a swivel. The faces of the pyramid were covered with the pictures of missionaries. When she could not sleep in the night, she turned to her missionaries and prayed for hours for the needs of the world. Together they were remarkably well-informed. From the newspaper, the radio, the television, and letters they kept abreast of what was happening. They prayed for kings and governments, for councils and mayors, for school superintendents and police chiefs.

One day when we stopped to see her, she was almost ecstatic with joy. She had heard a man speak over the radio and felt that doctrinally he lacked sound teaching. She had no way to get to him, except to pray that God would somehow show him his error. The doorbell had rung that afternoon, and the radio speaker stood on the doorstep as a visitor. He had heard of this remarkable bed-ridden woman through a friend and felt he should call. He was as pleased as she when she shared the story of her concern. Mother Cranston did not physically leave her house for years, and yet families, individuals, society itself felt the impact of her ministry, and some of them were prayed to her front door.

Jesus said, "Men ought always to pray and not to faint." We live in a day when people have hearts failing from fear. Tensions in the school. The breakdown of moral codes. Increase in crime. Why not have a ministry of praying, instead of complaining!

In many ways it is easier to pray with someone than alone. Your spiritual life and ministry will grow if you find a compatible prayer-partner. It's something to ask God for. Meeting regularly to pray with a friend for your personal needs and hers will provoke the kind of honest sharing that will bring you both closer to the Lord. You will be simply astounded at what will happen as you talk to God together.

Recently a woman shared with me her concern for a daughter who was rebellious and operating in open warfare against her parents. We talked about some possible causes that might be eliminated, because practical objective wisdom is part of our ministry to others. But then I asked if she and her husband, both of whom claimed to know God, could spend fifteen minutes every evening praying for their daughter. Her eyes dropped, she hesitated and was reluctant. Her attitude showed where some of the problem was. I suggested she begin praying that they could pray!

A quiet ministry comes from what we are. God is always more concerned about what we are than what we do. And if we are self-centered and shallow, petty and critical, then we need to pull handfuls of weeds from the garden so some other plants can flourish. God's promises are not to the slothful and negligent. He expects us to become. There are women who minister unconsciously to others out of a wealth of good thinking. They make it their business to read the right books, to appreciate what is worthwhile, while at the same time living with the problems of a real world. In other words, they have it put together. Life, that is.

Women need to "nourish their souls with good works, give it peace in solitude, get it strength in prayer, make it wise with reading, enlighten it by meditation, make it tender with love, sweeten it with psalms and hymns, and comfort it with frequent reflections upon future glory."[1] You may ask, Who has time for that? We had better find time along the way and order our priorities. Our older years will be as rich as we are making them today. Almost everyone has some luxury to meditate and love and sing and reflect—and even read and have some solitude—if they plan it that way. Why else do we have all these wonderful labor-saving devices in our homes? It's awesome, but you will be forever what you are becoming today.

Gifts obviously vary greatly in the exercising of ministry. The Bible speaks of this realistically, and says that in the body the greater parts cannot say they do not need the lesser parts. It is only as everyone ministers that the needs of the whole body are met. The challenge in exercising a gift in the ministry is to do for others rather than to do for self-gratification. The musician who wants to minister to others will keep the needs of her audience in mind. Otherwise she may show excellent voice control and a marvelous range, but there will be no ministry. Teachers do not teach subjects, they teach people, if they want to minister. *Home* makers make a home for people, not for the sake of perfection. Good cooks prepare food for enjoyment, not for praise.

I think of a diligent woman who volunteered to be in charge of the visual aid materials for a small school. She wanted a ministry. She became obsessed with the perfection of the materials and their arrangement. She worked very hard, and did an excellent job. But she became possessive. Procedures for the use of materials became so complicated that people stopped using them. She had a perfect department with no ministry. People are the point of any ministry, and we do well to remind ourselves of this.

Serving others ought to help us reach outside our own homes and families. We begin at home. Those who cannot minister to the people who are closest to them are unwilling to face the basic relationships of life. Their motivation is self-gratification, not ministry. It's not uncommon to find a woman who will involve herself deeply in a counseling ministry with others but won't listen to her own mother for more than five minutes. She is expansive with understanding for the stranger, but critical of her own family. There are many ways to hide from outreach to others. The married woman can hide behind her children and use them as an excuse for lack of involvement in the world. The single woman can hide behind her career and her fatigue, increasingly living an in-grown life. And neither of these may be aware of what they are doing.

I was so pleased when Alice moved into her own apartment. Now she could invite some of her single teacher friends home for a meal and hopefully a meaningful conversation. She had a place where she could initiate a Bible study. I knew some of the people with whom she taught and several were hurting inside and needed some love and understanding. But Alice didn't respond to either her apartment or God that way. Her concept of stewardship of possessions was nil, and she grew increasingly content to schedule her life around her television set. It was not until she went to a conference where a speaker honed in on the lordship of Christ that the veil came from before her eyes.

Opportunities to minister are thousand-fold. The neighborhood Bible study, or the study in the office. A good lending library, with enthusiasm for books. Transporting and working with handicapped children in a special program. Volunteer work at a hospital. Remembering to bring something small, but beautiful to a friend. Just plain thoughtfulness. Listening to others. Teaching a Sunday school class. Leading a study group. Helping in the kitchen. Some years ago I read about a Mrs. Ethel Miller in Washington State who heard of the need for surgical tools in mission hospitals. She began to wonder if doctors didn't collect more tools than they needed, just as she did in her kitchen. She called two doctors she knew, and they both had equipment they willingly donated. It began with a small project to help one mission hospital. Today she and a group of retired people ship enormous quantities of drug samples and surgical supplies to Africa and Asia. She's been doing this for years, since the day she first said "yes" to God when He prompted the idea.

We are whole people, and we need to see that ministry comes out of what we are. Now it's time to talk about our verbal witness to God's grace. In sharing the good news of salvation we are often tempted to pour truth over another's head. I have heard the phrase, "I gave her a witness," and wondered what that meant. Did it mean that she said something religious or gave a Scripture verse or what? How we live must support our words. We cannot avoid the discipline of having God work out His beauty in our lives, and when we share Jesus Christ with someone else it is in the context of this discipline.

The really Christian home is a great boon to sharing our faith. It is like a city set on a hill which cannot be hid. In any neighborhood when others observe a family trusting God, forgiving each other, affirming each other as people, living together in loving relationship, they take a second look: What does this family have? They see a "redemptive society" within the family, reflecting the reality of the Christian message.

The same thing takes place wherever people are truly Christian in their behavior patterns. Thoughtfulness, encouragement, helpfulness, a loving attitude—these all create a natural climate in which to share faith.

If what you believe means anything at all to you, you will find yourself speaking about it to others. You must speak. No one finds life in Christ simply by admiring the way you live. They must believe in Christ personally. Many non-Christians have healthy, whole ways to live, and unless you talk about your faith no one will be able to tell the difference.

Someone has defined sharing your faith as "one beggar telling another beggar where to find bread." I like that because it underscores the necessity for humility in sharing your faith. A redeemed sinner speaks, not a religious superior. If you "blow it" you can ask to be forgiven! Second, it emphasizes the need. People are lost, hungry, empty, dead in their sins without God. Some of them feel uneasy because they already suspect this is true; others have not begun to define their need. Having experienced what it means to be forgiven, to be made a member of God's family, you've got good news to share. You know what they need to know.

This necessitates your understanding the big picture of what the gospel really is all about. You want to communicate the heart of the message, without cultural trimmings, in a way that makes sense. And it does make sense. Man feels alienated from God. He can either try to rationalize why this is so, or he can come to terms with the holiness of God, the sinfulness of man, the meaning of the death of Christ, and what it means to live a Christian life under the lordship of Christ. But people have to hear the message in order to believe.

Hearing can come in a variety of settings. You can invite someone to church, but that is less personal and can make the person feel self-conscious. Someone may ask, "What do you believe?" which gives you a free opportunity to share. But more often we need to take time, to invest ourselves in communication which maximizes the person's opportunity to understand. Learn to ask questions. Jesus did this all the time. A good question can set in motion a whole process of understanding the inadequacy of unbelief and the sensibility of belief. If you are alert you will find that everyday conversation affords many opportunities for such questions or the remark which provokes a further query from your friend. We need to learn how to relax, be honest, and speak openly. The natural witness is more effective than the contrived, and we are not in this alone. God cares about other people far more than we do. He has invested the life of His Son in their redemption. He simply asks us to share the message.

Small group Bible studies provide a natural setting for learning and sharing together. Three or four—and certainly no more than ten—discussing a passage of Scripture can be like dynamite in individual lives. Ask, don't tell. Use a good discussion guide that insists that you go back to the biblical text to discover what it is saying. Groups like these in neighborhoods, in schools, in offices, and in homes are changing people. Those involved are experiencing the joy of sharing their own faith. This works for the married, the single, teenagers—wherever people are prepared to think.

The potential for our ministry is the potential found in the heart of a creative God. We need to say, "May I?" to God, not "Must I?" And if our will is set on reaching out, our faith will take us beyond the obstacles or difficulties we see. The willing heart, the full to overflowing heart—the possessors of these have an influence all out of proportion to their person. How pathetic to come in close contact with many lives and to have made no notable difference to others. Influencing others is inevitable when we have furnished our spirits with good things.

My favorite poet, Luci Shaw, expresses my own heart in her poem Hundredfold.

Yesterday
(after first frost, with maples
blazing beyond fringes of stubble hay)
my husband and my sons
pulled up dead summer's stalks of corn
laying them flat among the weeds
for plowing in again when next spring's born.

I'm glad I picked the green tomatoes
two nights ago
and spread them, newspapered
to ripen on the basement floor
good company for the corn relish, row
and golden row in jars behind the closet door.

*Silver Bells and Cockle Shells*

Yes, I'm very glad
something's left—something not dead
after all the hilling and hoeing
seeding and sprouting, greening and growing—
after the blowing
tassels high as a woman's hand above her head.

Corn relish for Sunday dinner—grace
the days when outside snowings
whiten winter's face!

Let me leave fruit
(but not in someone's basement)
when I grow browned
and old and pulled up by the root
and laid down flat
and ploughed into the ground.[2]

# II

·  ———  ·

# FREEDOM

One misty, cold Sunday morning in the northwoods she came into my life as a visitor from a nearby resort. Her name was Lisa, a Vassar student, and she had recently met the first real Christians she had ever known. They told her about our camping program for university students, and so she had come. It was time for morning worship, and I invited her into the lodge for the service.

She took in the student participation with relaxed and casual interest. But as the speaker began to read she strained forward as if to drink in every phrase. He read, "But the fruit of the Spirit is

>love
>joy
>peace
>patience
>kindness
>goodness
>faithfulness
>gentleness
>self-control."

He let each quality drop as a gem to be admired as he read. As quickly as the list was finished she turned to me with brimming eyes, gripped my arm, and said in a loud whisper, "That's what it is. That's what makes them so special!"

Looking at that cluster of fruit, she thought not of abstract ideas, but of two people. Those words described the Christians she had met. And the compelling quality of their lives made Lisa eager to know the source of such inner beauty. Small wonder she had said of them, "They are nice to know!"

The fruit of the Spirit never looked more winsome than during my talk with Lisa. Since then I have turned many times to Galatians 5, to read these verses in their context. The chapter begins: "It is for freedom that Christ has set us free. Stand firm, then, and do not let yourselves be burdened again by a yoke of slavery." The subject is freedom. Christ has set us free—free to have this kind of fruit in our lives: Love. Joy. Peace. Patience. Kindness. Goodness. Faithfulness. Gentleness. Self-control.

That is freedom worth talking about. Not just a freedom to talk about, but a freedom to experience, to have worked out at the core of life. Not an abstract idea, but a reality which others can identify.

What is this freedom Christ offers? It is the freedom of acceptance with God. No one has to work his way to the divine; God comes Himself to take away our guilt and graciously call us to Himself. Upon our individual response to Him, we are released from slavery and made His dear children, given all the family privileges.

Why would anyone experiencing such freedom from bondage be warned against submitting again to a yoke of slavery? It does seem absurd. But so easily we take back the management of our own affairs. We stop believing; we stop obeying. Our humanness gets in the way and pulls our eyes from God's supply to our own resources. We begin filling our own needs. Somehow, we believe we have to be good enough to make it to God. We've accepted His standard now, which makes performance even harder. Bondage.

Falling away from freedom into bondage is one problem. The Bible mentions another. It talks about freedom which leads to license. We're forgiven, we're accepted. We're free, aren't we? Let's do our own thing. The Bible calls this "using your freedom to indulge the sinful nature"—freedom as a launching pad for selfishness. How quickly freedom can fall into the pit of selfishness, distorted and twisted, bearing no likeness to the freedom to which we've been called.

The freedom Christ has given us is the freedom to reach our highest potential. Paul wrote earlier in this Galatian letter of his longing "that Christ be formed in you!" or "until you take the shape of Christ" (NEB). That is our potential, and we are not passive participants in this likeness to Christ.

The battleground is within us. Freedom is ours; but slavery is also a choice. Paul says, "Live by the Spirit and you will not gratify the desires of the sinful nature. For the sinful nature desires what is contrary to the Spirit, and the Spirit what is contrary to the sinful nature. They are in conflict with each other, so that you do not do what you want" (Galatians 5:16-17). He is talking about a realistic inner conflict. Christians possess two natures. The sinful nature is what we have by natural birth; the Spirit is the Holy Spirit who causes us to be "born again," to come alive spiritually. He is the One who indwells us. These two, the sinful nature and the Spirit, oppose each other in what has been called an "irreconcilable antagonism." Certainly as we learn to "walk by the Spirit" our old nature is increasingly subdued, but this comes by daily commitment, through daily right choices.

What is the choice I must make? I must decide who will direct my life—my sinful nature or the Holy Spirit. It is not self-effort that keeps us on track, but the Holy Spirit. It is yielding to Him. Without Him we end up with the works of the flesh instead of the fruit of the Spirit. Works versus fruit. The fruit comes from having our roots deep into the refreshment of God. He produces the fruit.

In contrast, the works of the flesh are obvious (Galatians 5:19-21): "Sexual immorality, impurity and debauchery; idolatry and witchcraft; hatred, discord, jealousy, fits of rage, selfish ambition, dissensions, factions and envy; drunkenness, orgies, and the like."

Contrasting *the works* and *the fruit* ought to sufficiently discipline our lives. Who would choose works to fruit? Yet there are some people whose lives are a constant round of ups and downs. Defeat and victory, depending on who is in control. The Bible says there is only one way to handle the problem. Those who belong to Christ Jesus have crucified the sinful nature with its passions and desires" (Galatians 5: 24).

*Crucified* is no half measure. It is pitiless and painful. It is decisive action. We nail our hangups to the cross, our poor, base desires which get us in trouble, and we leave them there. John Stott amplifies the significance of this by pointing out that death by crucifixion is not sudden, but gradual. While our old desires may often rear their heads, they have been nailed to the cross and we are determined to keep them there until they die.

The great secret of the Christian life is the decisiveness of our intention. Some people never intend to obey the gospel by submitting to the Lord. They try to arrange life so they can admit to the truth of Christianity without giving up themselves. They come again and again for counsel, for forgiveness; they may seek out psychiatrists or medical doctors for woes of the mind and flesh caused by their inability to give up. They need to decide to obey God by letting the Spirit control their lives.

You can think of a dozen illustrations from your own life, and so can I. Amy, for instance, had a problem with drugs. She started out "cool," just wanting a bit of a lift for her spirits, and ended up flat out and suicidal. She was invited to come to God for help and forgiveness. She struggled and kicked all the way and eventually went through the motion of giving her life to Christ. Her conversion seemed genuine, but as time went on she took out all her "works of the sinful nature" and handled them again to see if they were dead. They weren't. Her ups were less frequent than her downs. She was fitful, restless. Clearly she was not letting the Spirit direct her life. A confrontation was essential. Was she serious or not in her intent to give her life to Christ?

Only God knows when she really became His own child, but it was not until she abandoned herself to God that she began to develop the inner decisiveness to make choices that led to walking by the Spirit. Amy had never really given up her secret love for the weakness of her sinful nature. Drugs and sex still were an alive appeal that needed to be crucified. She could not crucify them by herself. When she gave herself completely, nothing held back, God captured her affection and gave her the help she needed.

The Spirit-controlled life is not fake role-playing. One person may have a well-developed personality and enough savvy to know how to live with others and thus be quite pleasant company. Another may grit his teeth and try to produce synthetic love and joy, in spite of poor digestion and many conflicts, in order to get along with others. Some may even enroll in charm courses hoping to become fascinating women. Others learn how to manage situations psychologically, taking apart the components of actions and conversations for analysis—and so managing life.

But this is self-effort, not the work of the Spirit in a person. In daily situations we have two choices: to handle it on our own, or to let the Spirit direct us. As we choose the latter, He works out a cluster of fruit in our life. I mention a cluster because the Bible doesn't say *fruits,* it says *fruit.* It's all of one piece. I can't say, Lord, I'll have a lot of love and joy, but forget about the faithfulness and self-control. Or I like apples and pears, but forget about plums. It is not *fruits,* but *fruit.* Each is attached to the other. It's the total picture of godly character.

Each characteristic mentioned reflects the character of God Himself. Love, joy, peace. He is the source of each, and it is His activity in our lives that produces genuine love, genuine joy, and genuine peace. Wouldn't you like to hang a sign on your door reading, "LOVE, JOY, PEACE LIVE HERE"? What a beautiful trio to have embodied in a person! We've already discussed God's kind of love and the meaning of joy in other chapters. But peace alone could fill a book. Peace with God. The peace of God. Peace: possession of adequate resources. Peace: the absence of conflict. Peace comes from what we know about God, not from what we know about ourselves. Shalom is a Hebrew greeting. Did this originate with God's activity in revealing Himself and His plan of redemption?

Every household should have the quality of *shalom.* It makes home a safe place. But it must come from your own heart as the tangible part of the fruit of the Spirit. Peace is not just an abstract ideal; it is a valid experience. Children are touched by peace, and so is everyone else. A boy once remarked about his mother, "She makes me quieter inside."

*Patience* is another translation for longsuffering. It means "steady under pressure." How patient God is with us! I remember a woman taking me to lunch one day and asking,

"If Gerald doesn't change by the end of the year, don't you think it would be okay for me to go ahead and get a divorce?" No one had ever asked me that question before and it left me a bit speechless. But then God provided the answer in my mind, "I think you can be as hard on Gerald as God has been on you." Longsuffering. God knows what that is about. It is inherent to His nature. He gives mercy upon mercy.

How many times has a woman thrown herself across the bed and cried out, "God, I can't take it any more. It's too much!" And God has come with a fresh supply of patience to cope with a hyperkinetic child, a poor job situation, a physical weakness—or whatever your heartache is. Longsuffering or patience isn't always what we want, but it is what we need from God, from others, and for our own character. God says that His patience and forbearance is meant to lead men to repentance. Will not He use our longsuffering to that end as well? It is called *longsuffering,* not endless suffering.

And what can be said of *kindness* and *goodness?* When we see these in action we appreciate afresh what it means to be human and made in the image of God. Our need and our aspirations are bound into one.

*Faithfulness* deserves a whole chapter in a day when vows are easily broken and the whimsy of our hearts leads us to rationalize our inconstancy. Faithfulness reflects God's heart. All of His character is in perfect harmony. We do not have to wonder if today He will be the same as He was yesterday. Will He keep His promise today? Yes. God is faithful.

He wants His children to be like Him. That is why He gave so many instructions about paying a vow, about "swearing to your own hurt and changing not." Did you say you would go? Then go. Did you say you would do it? Then do it. Faithfulness means that you can count on a person's integrity. She will not change when she has given her word.

Faithfulness is so rare today that it may become the Spirit's most convincing characteristic in our lives. Look at the Ten Commandments and observe how many are related to faithfulness—faithfulness in relationships, faithfulness in concern, faithfulness to God.

Some time ago a woman very dear to me left her husband, assuring me that God had told her this was all right because it had been a mistake in the first place. She felt nothing for him at this time. No unsolvable problems marred their marriage. She just preferred life without him. She *felt* a certain way. I protested on the basis of the character of God. What could she find in him that would allow her to be so faithless? She would not talk about God's character or her responsibility. She talked about how she felt. The fruit of the spirit is faithfulness—based on a commitment, based on righteousness, based on the character of God. We cannot claim to walk in the Spirit and be unfaithful.

The Spirit will keep us faithful, and because His fruit is one piece, He will fill us with love, joy, peace, patience, kindness, goodness. Faithfulness will not mean barrenness! It will mean godliness.

*Gentleness.* In a brusque world, what a lovely gem. No arrogance, no guile in gentleness. The gentle person hears a voice outside herself, and sees a person through the eyes of the Creator. Gentleness forgets self because of concern for others.

*Self-control.* I listened to an angry woman who couldn't find her off-switch, and thus went on and on, raising her blood pressure and irritating everyone else's gastric juices. Such a small, stupid thing set her off. I wondered if she could be that angry over genuine injustice and evil!

I talked to a young woman, newly married, who had trouble doing anything unpleasant because she had never in her life had to do what she didn't want to do. She couldn't discipline her life to have any order. She was always behind with mountains of work undone, agreed upon responsibilities that were not completed. Previously her sexual attractiveness had made the man in her life overlook things that her best girlfriends could have warned him about, but now he was no longer moved by her coquettish behavior. How do you make yourself do what you don't want to do? she asked. Do it with God's help. The fruit of the Spirit is self-control.

When things don't go right, when they go unexpectedly very wrong: self-control. It's bigger than biting your tongue, or learning to cool it. It is the Spirit's inner-working of peace inside you. Self-control is the opposite of circumstance-control.

Dr. Donald Grey Barnhouse put it this way: "Love is the key. Joy is love singing. Peace is love resting. Longsuffering is love enduring. Kindness is love's touch. Goodness is love's character. Faithfulness is love's habit. Gentleness is love's self-forgetfulness. Self-control is love holding the reins." And if we go on to say that God is love, we have tied the cord of God's character around this cluster of fruit.

As I read this list of the fruit of the Spirit, I long more and more to have this worked out in my daily life. It is the heart of being a Christian woman. The resources of God are available to live this kind of a life, but we are slow to take them. It's hard to keep within a budget. We overspend in almost every area of life except this one. If we believe, says Bishop Houghton, why do we live so far below our spiritual income?

Let me suggest two poor attitudes that cause spiritual paralysis and keep us from moving on with God. (l) We may have unrealistic expectations that defeat us before we even begin. Being human gives us an in-built tendency to blame others for their imperfections and the distress this causes us. We keep waiting for things to change, so we can begin to grow spiritually. Sometimes we try a self-improvement course because we blame ourselves for everything that has gone wrong, and we want to get ourselves in shape to begin to trust God.

The world isn't perfect, our family isn't perfect, our friends aren't perfect, we aren't perfect. None of this takes God by surprise. Why it should surprise sinners that they are imperfect is a mystery. But some women can't believe that God has done much until the situation becomes absolute perfection—which it hardly ever does on earth. For instance, a mother can keep peace from flowing through her home while she waits for everyone to shape up. I know of a woman who fussed because her husband stopped at the tavern every night on his way home from work. When he stopped doing that she fussed because he didn't come to the table at her first call for supper. She forgot all about thanking God that the tavern was no longer an issue.

Another woman I know prayed that God would help her daughter become a better student at school. When the daughter's attitude changed and she moved up to a C average, the mother kept pushing and praying that she would become an A student. Kathleen was not made to be an A student; she was a loving, kind C student. Her mother had unrealistic goals based on her view of how things ought to be rather than on how they actually were. No love, joy, or peace came through from this mother to the family because the fruit of the Spirit wasn't realized in her own life. She didn't recognize God's help when she saw it.

The Christian woman needs to learn to live in a real

world, with real problems, with a real God who is capable of meeting our human needs for time and eternity. And she needs to set time against eternity to keep her values straight. In light of eternity much of what we count of supreme worth will be seen as trivia.

A Christian woman gives all she knows of herself to all she knows of God and continues to grow in the knowledge of both. She becomes a channel for the outflow of His character as she takes on "the shape of Christ." She cannot wait for life to change, but says "The life I now live, I live by faith."

(2) We may have an inadequate concept of freedom which makes us afraid to give ourselves completely to anyone, least of all to God. The key to giving ourselves to others is our personal abandonment to God. But we are afraid. And so we hold on tightly to ourselves, afraid to lose our life because we are bent on saving it.

Freedom involves living the way we were intended to live, according to our nature. For instance, a train is constructed to run on rails. It experiences freedom only when it accepts the limitations that its nature imposes on it. A train going along the track at full speed is a wonderful sight, but a train attempting to cross a plowed field is a disaster.

Just so with a pianist who accepts the discipline of the keyboard. Her greatest flights of freedom and self-expression are not in defiance of this discipline, but in submission to it.

Who best knows the nature of our freedom? I would sooner give God that wisdom than claim it for myself. Bishop Frank Houghton once commented that ever since Isaiah had seen the Lord sitting upon a throne, high and lifted up, he had known it was absolutely safe to trust Him. Every woman needs that kind of confrontation with God. Only then can she fully abandon herself, and find that in losing her life she saves it. When she lets go and casts herself on the goodness of

God, then she will know the meaning of freedom. C. S. Lewis has said, "Until you have given your self to Him you will not have a real self." She who loses her life shall find it!

A persuaded heart. That is what it means to have faith. And that faith releases "the refreshing energies of God" on our behalf. No position of power, no possessions of this world, no honors or achievements can compare with it. A persuaded heart is a woman's peace and power.

## Footnotes

### Chapter 3

[1] "The Road Not Taken" from *The Poetry of Robert Frost,* edited by Edward Connery Lathem, Copyright 1916. Copyright 1969 (Holt, Rinehart and Winston). Copyright 1944 by Robert Frost. Reprinted by permission of Holt, Rinehart and Winston.

[2] Anne Bernay, *Atlantic,* March 1970, p. 107.

[3] Paul Tournier, *The Adventure of Living* (1965, Harper & Row) p. 236.

### Chapter 4

[1] C. S. Lewis, *The Silver Chair* (1953, Macmillan) p.16. Reprinted with permission of The Macmillan Company.

### Chapter 5

[1] Clyde S. Kilby, "The Aesthetic Poverty of Evangelicalism."

[2] *Honey for a Child's Heart* (1969, Zondervan).

### Chapter 6

[1] Joseph Bayly, *Psalms of My Life* (1987, Tyndale). Used by permission.

### Chapter 10

[1] William Law, *A Serious Call to a Devout and Holy Life* (1945, Westminster) p. 38.

[2] Luci Shaw, *Listen to the Green* (Harold Shaw). Used by permission.

# NOTE TO THE READER

The publisher invites you to share your response to the message of this book by writing Discovery House Publishers, P. O. Box 3566, Grand Rapids, MI 49501, U.S.A., or by calling 1-800-283-8333. For information about other Discovery House publications, contact us at the same address and phone number.